Half our life is spent trying to find something to do with the time we have rushed through life trying to save.
Will Rogers

There is one insuperable obstacle to a belief in ghosts. A ghost never comes naked: he appears either in a winding-sheet or "in his habit as he lived." To believe in him, then, is to believe that not only have the dead the power to make themselves visible after there is nothing left of them, but that the same power inheres in textile fabrics. Supposing the products of the loom to have this ability, what object would they have in exercising it? And why does not the apparition of a suit of clothes sometimes walk abroad without a ghost in it? These be riddles of significance. They reach away down and get a convulsive grip on the very tap-root of this flourishing faith.
Ambrose Bierce

Ghosts seem harder to please than we are; it is as though they haunted for haunting's sake -- much as we relive, brood, and smolder over our pasts.
Elizabeth Bowen

Of all ghosts, the ghosts of our old loves are the worst.
Sir Arthur Conan Doyle

The murdered do haunt their murderers, I believe. I know that ghosts have wandered on earth. Be with me always -- take any form -- drive me mad! Only do not leave me in this abyss, where I cannot find you!
Emily Bronte

The ghosts you chase you never catch.
John Malkovich

My utterance is mighty, I am more powerful than the ghosts; may they have no power over me.
Egyptian Book of the Dead

Over 100 Years of Oklahoma's Haunted History

GHOSTLAHOMA

TONYA HACKER
& TAMMY WILSON

- A Whitechapel Productions Press Book from Dark Haven Entertainment -

This Book is Dedicated to:
Tonya's children, Tegan Breanna and Airis Lindsey, and Tammy's children, Bailey, Madison, Peyton, and Wyatt. We are forever grateful for their company on all their "adventures" and love them dearly.

© Copyright 2009 by Tonya Hacker & Tammy Wilson
All Rights Reserved, including the right to copy or reproduce this book,
or portions thereof, in any form, without express permission from the author and publisher

Original Cover Artwork Designed by
© Copyright 2008 by Michael Schwab & Troy Taylor
Visit M & S Graphics at http://www.manyhorses.com/msgraphics.htm

This Book is Published By:
Whitechapel Press
A Division of Dark Haven Entertainment, Inc.
15 Forest Knolls Estates - Decatur, Illinois - 62521
(217) 422-1002 / 1-888-GHOSTLY
Visit us on the internet at http://www. dark haven entertainment. com

First Printing -- February 2009
ISBN: 1-892523-64-7

Printed in the United States of America

FOREWORD

We all enjoy a good spine-tingling ghost story, especially those that are true. For these are the tales that keep us wondering about them long after the last page has been read. As a writer of true regional ghost stories, I'm always delighted to read the work of others. What better way to learn about an area, especially if one happens to be a ghost aficionado? As a historian and paranormal researcher, I know the long hours of work involved in completing such a book as Ghostlahoma. No one could have done it any better than Oklahoma's own Tammy Wilson and Tonya Hacker.

It's one thing to write a book about a location's haunted happenings. It's a different matter entirely to know whereof one writes. These two ladies do. Both are seasoned paranormal investigators. They've paid their paranormal dues in haunted locations all across the Sooner State. Just try to slip phony evidence past one of them. Good luck. You'll need it! This feisty duo will quickly point out the error of your ways. They know their stuff. And it shows in every tale presented here in Ghostlahoma. Avid historians with a wealth of knowledge about Oklahoma, Tammy and Tonya will charm you with their writing style. No two ways about it. Among my favorite stories are the historical "Bricktown Banshees" and "Vina Rae's Grill and Graze." Who killed Ann Reynolds and why? Snuggle in, get good and comfortable; you're in for a real treat with Ghostlahoma.

Janice Oberding
Author, *The Haunting of Las Vegas*

TABLE OF CONTENTS

OKLAHOMA'S FIRST GHOST STORY - Page 8
Originally printed in The Guthrie Daily Leader - 1896, Discovered by Tonya Hacker

THE FRISCO BAR - By Tammy Wilson -- Page 11

GHOST ON AISLE THREE? - Submitted by Mark Keefer -- Page 12

THE PURPLE CHURCH - By Tonya Hacker -- Page 13

THE DEVIL HOUSE - By Tammy Wilson and Shirley McCoy -- Page 15

THE BLACK JAIL - By Tonya Hacker -- Page 17

VINA RAE'S GRILL & GRAZE - By Tammy Wilson -- Page 21

THE SKIRVIN HOTEL - By Tonya Hacker -- Page 25

FROM DADDY - Submitted by Shirley McCoy -- Page 33

CLAY HALL - By Tammy Wilson -- Page 34

THE LITTLE LOST GIRL - Submitted by Elizabeth S. Tyree -- Page 36

JUST A DREAM? - Submitted by Beth Reaves -- Page 38

A HAUNTING IN HUGO - By Tonya Hacker -- Page 42

THE UNEARTHING OF SOMETHING WEIRD IN THE BEAVER SANDS (THE TRUE STORY OF THE BEAVER SANDS PORTAL, ALSO KNOWN AS THE SHAMAN'S PORTAL) - By Tammy Wilson -- Page 46

THE LADY IN BLACK - Submitted by Roxanne Geddes -- Page 52

A STORMY NIGHT IN ADA - Submitted by Regina Walker -- Page 53

THE SMITH HOUSE - By Tammy Wilson -- Page 54

TRICK OR TREAT - Submitted by Penn King -- Page 57

OKLAHOMA'S OWN DEAD MAN'S CURVE - Anonymous -- Page 59

ELKS LODGE NO. 743 - By Tonya Hacker -- Page 61

GRANNY'S HOUSE - By Tammy Wilson -- Page 65

OKLAHOMA'S PHANTOM HITCHHIKERS - By Tonya Hacker -- Page 69

GRANDMA'S HOUSE - Submitted by Lana Billings -- Page 75

A VERY "TOUCHING" EXPERIENCE - Submitted by Jason Clark -- Page 76

SURETY ABSTRACT - By Tammy Wilson -- Page 77

THE COLD ROOM - Submitted by Mark Keefer -- Page 79

WOODWARD MEMORIAL HOSPITAL - By Tammy Wilson -- Page 81

GHOSTLY ZIPPO - Submitted by James Bradley -- Page 85

A HAUNT AT THE HOSPITAL - Submitted by Russell White -- Page 90

THERE'S A MONSTER IN THE CLOSET - Anonymous -- Page 91

EVERYONE KNOWS THE MUSEUM IS HAUNTED - By Tammy Wilson -- Page 94

SOMEONE TO WATCH OVER ME? - Submitted by Samara Stephenson -- Page 92

THE PASSENGER - Submitted by David McCoy -- Page 94

SPIRITS OF SAPULPA - Anonymous -- Page 96

BRICKTOWN BANSHEES - By Tonya Hacker -- Page 97

A HOUSE IN GARBER - Anna Groom -- Page 107

THE OLD FARMHOUSE - Anonymous -- Page 109

MURDER THREE TIMES - By Tammy Wilson -- Page 110

A LOST FRIEND, GHOST TRACKS, AND A SPOOK IN THE NIGHT - By Tammy Wilson and Shirley McCoy -- Page 113

A HAUNTING ON TYLER STREET - Anonymous -- Page 115

MARY'S HOUSE - By Tammy Wilson -- Page 117

DEAD WOMAN'S CROSSING - By Troy Taylor -- Page 119

THE CARMEN HOME - By Tammy Wilson -- Page 123

ABOUT THE AUTHORS -- Page 127

INTRODUCTION: OKLAHOMA'S FIRST GHOST STORY DISCOVERED

Since this is our first book about ghosts and hauntings in Oklahoma, we found it only fitting to include the first documented Oklahoma ghost story. This story was found at the Guthrie Historical Society and as far as they have been able to discern, it is the first written documentation of a ghost story in Oklahoma. This shows how times have changed; it is highly unlikely that a daily newspaper would report on a haunting these days, but at the time this was documented, it was the news. Enjoy...

The Guthrie Daily Leader - 1896:
NO INQUEST NEEDED. ELLA MYERS' ASSOCIATES WERE THE CAUSE OF HER HASTY BURIAL!
*Thursday, April 9, 1896 *

(Note: Cyprian is another word for prostitute) Commissioner Stapleton says he is in no way responsible for the hasty burial of Ella Myers, the Cyprian who was found dead Sunday inside Ella Horton's place on the Santa Fe right of way. He says he issued an order for her burial as a pauper on authority of Coroner Barker, who, with Dr. Cotteral examined the remains.

The county undertaker, it seems, complied with the inmates of the Huston place and buried the body at once. Dr. Barker says he gave an order for the burial of the body, which was badly decomposed, but had no idea the undertaker would act so hastily. Dr. Cotteral does not credit the story that the body was buried alive. He says he applied the galvanic battery, and like Dr. Barker thought an inquest was unnecessary, as it would simply heap expenses on the county. The deceased was a cocaine fiend and died from an overdose, so the doctors say.

RED HAND APPEARED. HOUSE IN WHICH A CYPRIAN DIED SAID TO BE HAUNTED!
*April 15, 1896 *
The shack on the Santa Fe right of way in which the Cyprian Lula [sic]

Myers recently died is haunted. Horrible groans issue from the shack every night and passerby assert that weird and ghastly incantations take place within the building, which was vacated shortly after the unfortunate girl's death. Last night a well-known sport called at the house and tried the front door. It failed to give way. He tried the back door with the same result, and returning to the front door it suddenly flew open and a blood-red hand holding a vial appeared in the room. Much excitement prevails among the neighbors residing in the vicinity of the haunted house.

THE GHOST STILL WALKS! ELLA MYERS HAUNTS THOSE WHO INJURED HER. IS HER BODY UPSIDE DOWN?
*Sunday April 19, 1896 *

Judge McCord believes that an investigation will reveal some startling things. George Hardies's weird experience at the home of the deceased Cyprian.

A Blood Red Hand Seen

The ghost of Ella Myers continues to walk with uncanny tread at the errs-while [sic] dive at the Santa Fe right of way. Last night at 12 o clock the doors of the house in which the girl is supposed to have died suddenly flew open and a figure clad in white was seen at the window. It is alleged that the groans also issued from the hitherto locked house, and that three times a plaintive wail went up: "Don't give me any morphine I am sick!" for over a week super natural manifestations in the house have aroused the neighborhood, and the shacks in the vicinity of the haunted dwelling have been vacated.

On Friday night, George Hardie, thinking the story of the ghost was a prime josh, called at the house. He found the front door locked. Going to the back door he found it locked and bolted. Hardie went to the front door, and was preparing to return, disgusted, to town, when a low plaintive wail assailed his ears and almost simultaneously the front doors slowly swung open. Although, badly rattled, Hardie entered the house. In the room where the Myers girl died he was struck four sharp raps on the head, and at the same time a light, resembling a calcium ray flashed across the room, and within the ray appeared a blood-red hand clutching a bottle or a phial. Manifestations and ghostly séances similar to those seen and heard by Hardie have been experienced by twenty-five or thirty persons who have visited the dwelling out of curiosity.

Kickapoo Charley visited the place Thursday and was badly frightened. In fact he fainted after seeing the apparition, and had been ill ever since.

Ex-Police Judge McCord is considerably wrought up over the appearance of the astral body. He adheres to the belief that the Myers girl was buried alive and that the body was chucked into a coarse box face downwards.

Policeman Potete avers that the exhuming of the body of the

unfortunate Cyprian will show that the body is distorted and twisted, and that the girl's ghost will haunt the colored undertaker, and her associates as long as they live. The brother of the dead girl is in the city, and will have the body disinterred and moved to Kansas for burial. It is thought he knows more about the strange case than he tells.

Also in the same paper:

DIE A PAUPER AND BE CHUCKED INTO A HOLE ON THE COTTONWOOD!

"If you have no money and wish a decent burial when you die, postpone dying until you get out of Logan County," remarked a prominent businessman yesterday. "I have just returned from a ride about town," he continued, "and during my rounds I passed by what is supposed to be the burial ground for paupers. I must say such a graveyard is a burning disgrace to the county. A man who would place a dead body in that soggy plat of ground is devoid of all the merciful, humane feeling, which goes to make up a man. Surely the county has enough money to give its dead a respectful burial. This graveyard is a marsh on the Cottonwood. The county undertaker, after slapping a stiff into a box, hurries it to that wet marsh and deposits it about four feet under the ground. About twice a year the river rises and overflows the graves, and we drink the water. Why can't a plot of ground be staked off in Lynn's cemetery for the indigent dead? The county owes that much to decency's sake."

NO MORE GHOST! - THE REMAINS OF ELLA MYERS EXHUMED AND FOUND RIGHT SIDE UP!

*April 23, 1896 *

The remains of Ella Myers, whose ghost is said to have haunted the late home of the deceased on the Santa Fe right of way, were exhumed yesterday by H.M. Myers, half brother of the deceased, and taken to Rose Hill Township for interment. Mr. Myers was ignorant of the death of his sister until he read an account of the haunted house in the Leader last week. The coffin was opened and the body was found in proper position. It is intimated that the girl was not only buried alive, but the body was placed in a rough box face downward, but since the recent comment regarding her burial, interested parties disinterred the remains and placed them in their natural position.

There were no more mentions about "ghosts" by the Santa Fe right of way in the newspaper after April 1896.

THE FRISCO BAR

By Tammy Wilson

The oldest bar in Enid, open since 1948, is the Frisco Bar located at 608 N. Independence. It was originally down the street from its current location but that building is no longer there. The current building was a machine shop downstairs with a brothel upstairs. The Frisco is famous for its ice cold beer, but there are chilly spirits of another kind there, too.

A massive collection of beer bottles and cans lines the upper walls of the bar. One evening, the owner, Jim O'Neill, was standing behind the bar visiting with one of the customers when one beer bottle came flying several feet away from the shelf and nearly hit the customer at the bar. Now, keep in mind that these cans and bottles are nestled quite closely together on these shelves in tiers, but not one of them was disturbed by this one that seemingly propelled itself off the shelf. A picture has also fallen off the wall and onto the floor, and again, not one can or bottle was disturbed. O'Neill and his employees have witnessed the water faucet at the sink behind the bar turn on by itself as well.

They say the Frisco ghost is to blame for the flying objects and random water running. In the early morning hours one day, O'Neill and another man were in the bar. O'Neill had just returned from picking up the newspaper from the front sidewalk when his friend asked, "Didn't you lock that back door?" O'Neill assured him he had.

The man told him he had heard it open and said, "Someone just walked up that ramp to the men's room."

O'Neill wasn't too worried about it. "That's just the ghost," he told him. He reported that people often hear the back door open and when they look to see who's coming, they witness a black figure walking up the ramp toward the men's room. Though the origins of the ghost are unknown, O'Neill and some of the others are used to it by now. Some won't readily admit to believing in it, but will certainly clean up as quickly as they can when they're in the men's room alone.

GHOST ON AISLE THREE?

Submitted by Mark Keefer

In the late 1990s, I worked at Lowe's as a receiving manager. I used to have to get to work early to work on freight trucks and get things ready for the other employees. I was there most every morning at about 4 a.m. One morning, shortly after another manager, Kathy Daniels, and I had arrived, it started storming. It was a horrendous storm, one of those horribly loud early summer thunderstorms. Now, the way the Lowe's phone system worked was that before the store opened, all outside phone calls that came into the store would ring over the PA system so you could hear the phone ring from anywhere inside the store. Well, I was in the back of the store when I heard the phone ring in my office. This, of course, meant that it wasn't an outside phone call: it was coming from inside the store.

I could see Kathy, so I knew it wasn't her calling me. I ran to answer the phone, but the floor was slick and I slipped and fell. As I limped into my office, I looked at the caller ID. For in-store calls, you could tell where the call was coming from by looking at a chart we had. However, the number was one that I didn't recognize. I answered the call anyway. All I could hear was rain and then thunder. I could literally hear raindrops pounding into pavement and the low rumble of thunder in the receiver of the phone I was holding in my hand. I cross-referenced the number with my little chart on my desk and found the call was coming from a phone at a cash register out near our outside lawn and garden area. I said hello again... nothing. And then the line went dead.

By this time, Kathy was standing next to me and she could see the weird look on my face. I told her about the phone call and what I had heard and she just stared at me stone-faced. Suddenly, she turned white and gasped, "I just unlocked the doors to the garden center!" This meant that if there was anyone out there, standing in the rain messing with us, he now had full access to the entire store, and thus had access to us. I grabbed a piece of lumber (it was Lowe's after all) and she grabbed a shovel. We ran and relocked the doors. Then, as we were standing there we started hearing all sorts of bizarre noises coming from inside the store. We'd had enough by that point. We ran into the electrical room and turned virtually every light in the store on with the flip of a switch or two. All of the bright fluorescent bulbs were turned on. The marquee outside was turned on. All of the security lights were now on. It had to be a heck of a sight to see Lowe's glowing that brightly at 4:15 in the morning from Garriott Road.

Thankfully, we never found anything. Unfortunately, we've never been able to explain the incident, either.

THE PURPLE CHURCH

An Oklahoma Legend
By Tonya Hacker

Growing up in Oklahoma, tales of terror were a prominent teenage tradition. As an adult I now realize that young boys created a lot of these horrifying stories. High hopes of scaring girls into their arms were typically the culprits behind these types of legends. As an investigator I have witnessed many of what I now call "foundation legends." These are the legends that have nothing to claim other than an old concrete foundation or even a part of a basement. There is no structure left behind. Upon discovery of the concrete foundations you can expect to witness a lot of really tacky graffiti by kids who were obviously motivated by the heavy metal scene of the late 1980s, though some locations hold a firmer grasp to satanic lore, even quotes by infamous devil worshippers in history. I have found the foundation legends to be intriguing and slightly humorous over the years.

Most people assume the Purple Church was actually an old church building, painted purple of course. On the contrary, how this legend developed is still a mystery. This celebrated paranormal hot spot is just east of the Oklahoma City limits. Investigative teams from across the state have trampled through the back roads and weed-infested foliage to lay eyes on the legendary Purple Church. Many have located the token foundation while others have been chased away by what some reported as demonic rednecks ready to kill, shotgun-style. Those who have successfully located the unholy grounds of the Purple Church quickly realized that the land on which it sits is as unique as the neighbors in the area.

The tales of the disturbed past of this foundation and basement area are filled with secrecy and menace. Floating heads have been witnessed by passersby and mysterious balls of light appearing from nowhere have become common occurrences near the ruins of the old church. Accounts of evil doings, deadly rituals, and even human sacrifices have been branded into the land forever. Upon arriving at the location, people report piles of bones and dark ceremonial objects placed about. Disembodied voices are said to ascend from the dark, damp corridors of the legendary basement. A frequent paranormal claim is that animal and perhaps even human sacrifice has taken place in the pentagram-decorated tomb of death. Screams of anguish, and of course, dark shadows, guard the basement with sometimes-violent watchful eyes. Some tell tales of curious youngsters being pulled into the basement's bowels only to be later found dead. Earlier reports claim that the youngsters' bodies were positioned as if they had committed suicide during some satanic ritual. Some say their deaths were caused by supernatural demons in the business of collecting souls to join their church.

The Purple Church is just one of Oklahoma's renowned hot spots for paranormal activity. That is, of course, if you are brave enough to locate it. Rumors of the occult and deathly séances are unbridled in this particular spot. After speaking with some locals I have learned that the stories were possibly made up to keep teenagers off private property and to protect a cherished and highly illegal crop of supernatural herbs. No matter what the origin of the Purple Church is, it has caused many curious souls to venture out to discover if the legend is in fact real.

There is no doubt that such a foundation exists. To many a visit to the Purple Church it is a risk to be taken to prove that the tales are true once and for all. These types of foundation legends are very common across the United States. Perhaps you have a Purple Church in your town. Possibly you received your first kiss at a location that was filled full of spooky hazards and utterly frightening anecdotes. Such places are part of local legend and culture. Remember when you returned to school on Monday to relay your exaggerated ghostly experience to your friends? Do you recall the adrenaline rush you felt as you ran for your life from that screaming hell-bound banshee, also known as Mr. Owl? No matter what history says, the infamous Purple Church is a part of Oklahoma folklore. It is unproven but has stood the test of time in our great state. There is no need to search out this foundation haunting, unless you are willing to take a risk of being shot at or perhaps becoming one of the lost souls collected by the sinister phantoms of the Purple Church.

THE DEVIL HOUSE

By Shirley McCoy and Tammy Wilson

I was so excited! We were finally moving from our tiny cramped studio apartment into a roomy two-bedroom house with a yard for Tammy (our twelve-month-old) to play in. It was an older home and we had a lot of cleaning up to do to make it habitable.

Within weeks of moving in, odd things started to happen. At first they were just small things: a ceramic horse was moved from the TV cabinet to the fireplace mantle and the heavy leather recliner would be turned to face the corner (not being a swivel recliner it was difficult to move it in any direction.) Often, drawn shades would be opened and opened shades would be drawn shut. There were times I experienced strange and creepy feelings. But we were young and inexperienced and we didn't take these things too seriously. We laughed it off and joked that we probably had a poltergeist.

Things started to escalate and soon we were no longer laughing. One evening I went into the kitchen and was shocked to find all the cabinet doors and drawers hanging open. The forks and knives were stuck in the ceiling, dangling there ready to fall on any individual wandering in. It was no longer funny. The "feelings" became foreboding and I was very apprehensive about being alone in the house. To make matters worse, once a week Tammy's dad worked out of town leaving me as her sole protector. I had to lay my fears and anxieties aside and shelter her from any possible harm.

One night, around 3 a.m., I was abruptly awakened. I had been dragged halfway off the bed. I wasn't aware when it was happening but I suddenly found myself partially on the floor. Trembling, I jumped up to check on Tammy. My bedroom door was shut and the lights were on. Upon opening the door I found all the lights in the house were on. All the doors, cabinets, and drawers were flung open, the front and back door were wide open, and my St. Bernard was cowering under the dining table, whimpering.

I ran to Tammy, scooped her from her crib, grabbed her diaper bag and headed for the car. We found a well-lit parking lot and spent the rest of the night there. After returning home the next day I informed Tammy's dad of the events that had transpired the previous night. I then refused to return to that house. We hurriedly found another house and moved.

Eighteen years later, I was an employment counselor doing an intake on a new client. Seeing his address, I mentioned I had lived in that house at one time. He asked, "Anything weird ever happen to you there?"

***

Tammy: My mother and her client exchanged stories about the house and she found that he had been having the same strange things going on there nearly twenty years later.

I thought this was a great example of a haunted house since two completely unrelated people had things happen there, so I frequently related this story to friends during ghost story sessions. One evening I was telling the story to my friend who worked at a local pharmacy and when I mentioned the address, he became white as a ghost himself. He started pacing around the room, muttering frantically. I asked him what was wrong.

He said to me, "We used to deliver medicine to a lady that lived there and we always thought she was crazy because she was always going on about how the devil lived in her house!"

THE BLACK JAIL

214 Noble Ave.
Guthrie, Oklahoma
By Tonya Hacker

Fifteen years before statehood, the unassigned lands of Oklahoma were abundant with gunslingers, robbers, and notorious western symbols. In 1892 Guthrie, Oklahoma was home to one of the very first federal prisons in the Midwest.

Labeled the "Black Jail" by inmates, the eighteen-inch-thick walls of dark limestone and brick housed a penitentiary that was rumored to be escape-proof back in the days of the Wild West. Intimidating to the locals, the shadowy halls of this prison detained some of America's most notorious criminals of the day. Notorious outlaws such as the well-known Bill Doolin and his gang of murderous thieves frequently passed through the dank cells. The legendary Dalton Gang also had its last go 'round at the prison during its first years of operation.

The two-story structure housed ninety prisoners at a time. The two levels included a basement where the unruly convicts were held in solitary confinement, which was becoming a popular way to offer treatment to hardened criminals in hopes to cure them of their wrongful ways -- and in the long run offer the community a sense of safety. Living conditions at the prison were varied. While the local newspaper reports that harsh conditions were not the norm, other reports offer a different view. Lack of ventilation for the prisoners confined there was the main concern to many within the community. Being shut into small cells during the terrible Oklahoma heat and the harsh cold winters was not exactly a positive experience for the confined men during their incarceration time. The thought of escape was never far from the minds of the inmates wishing to seek refuge from the prison's

The Black Jail -- Oklahoma's First Territorial Prison

rough and occasionally deathly atmosphere. Local newspapers frequently reported escape attempts with fatal outcomes.

Subsequent to the prison closing in the early 1900s, the building housed a local chapter of the Nazarene Church. The church occupied the former prison building for many years. After the church closed in the late 1970s, the building sat unoccupied until the well-known Samaritan Foundation opened its doors to cult members who chose Guthrie, Oklahoma, as their new home. Locals were always unsure about the rituals being preformed in the church. It quickly became one of the things that shamed the town. Murder, scandal, and conspiracy were hastily associated with the Samaritan Foundation all the way up until 1995. The townspeople of Guthrie realized that the Foundation was not what they had thought it was. The Foundation headquarters were known to house and harbor anti-government activists and radicals, along with children and runaways. The doors were officially closed in the late 1990s after the Department of Human Services declared the structure to be unfit for the children who lived in the compound. The strange history of this building leaves no doubt that it may be inhabited by ghostly energy and unexplained occurrences that people witness today.

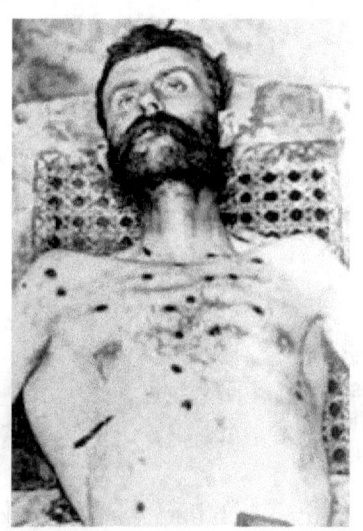

Bill Doolin and his gang passed frequently through the walls of the "Black Prison". He is seen here after being gunned down in Oklahoma.

Today, the prison is undergoing restoration and has been selected for preservation grants and federal money. It seems that supernatural and paranormal activity plagues the walls of the prison as workers and supporters of the restoration project report many odd occurrences. The edgy feeling of being followed, being solemnly watched by unseen eyes and the occasional haunting murmurs descending down the cell halls are a reminder of those who resided within the prison many years ago.

One of the most familiar spirits at the prison has been assumed to be the ghost of James Phillips. In June 1907, Phillips was the first white man sentenced to be hanged at the prison for the murder of a local man. According to the State Capital News Paper and prison records, Phillips was to die the very next morning across the street from Noble Avenue. As he kept watch out his cellblock window, he witnessed the carpenters as they hurriedly built his gallows. It was reported by guards that he was observing the construction with great dread when he abruptly fell backwards onto his bunk and died instantly without a sound. The coroner's report published in the local newspapers stated, "He simply died of fright."

The ghost of James Phillips has been reported to pace the corridors of the basement, nervously awaiting his hanging, unaware that he has passed on. Witnesses who pass by on the street have reported seeing a man peering out a lower level window. Workers and preservation volunteers have seen an unexplained dark shadow on occasion. This shadow seems to seek refuge in the cell where Phillips was rumored to have died that summer day almost 100 years ago. Is James Phillips still awaiting his death in the historic Black Jail? Is he unable to realize that he has already passed on and that he was, in fact, successful in avoiding the gallows?

One more ghostly tale is that of a young woman. No one is certain why she is present at the building and what time frame she fits into, but a witness account tells of a woman's voice heard singing throughout the main level of the building. The select few who have seen this ghost report that she is wearing a long printed dress, a large-brimmed hat and gloves, The woman has been noticed outside the prison walking the grounds and on occasion attempting to cross Noble Avenue. Drivers have been known to slow down or even stop in the middle of the road as she makes her way across and swiftly vanishes before stepping on the curb. Some locals believe she was a prostitute who would visit the prisoners to offer her services and provide leisure activity for those who displayed good behavior during their confinement. However, others believe that she was a prominent member of the Nazarene Church. As one witness stated, "She looked like a civilized woman, walking with her head high into the church doors." Remnants of the old church still hang suspended from the ceiling on the main floor of the building and rusted patterned tin tiles still lie on the floor of what used to be a sanctuary and worship hall.

The nameless woman appears only on occasion, usually at dusk. Whoever she is, or was, remains a mystery. The familiar residual haunting of her roaming the prison grounds, halls, and the road outside is something the locals have accepted as part of

the building's history.

While being able to research the location, and spend some time inside the walls of the prison, I personally experienced a few unexplainable moments. Walking the main floor of the prison, I noticed a large hole in the floor. I stopped walking to examine the hole only to hear footsteps lingering behind me. When I turned to see who it was, no one was there. Another time I was in the basement, photographing the rumored cell of James Phillips. I noticed a man walking past the window. In hopes that it was one of the volunteer workers, I rushed up the worn stairs to speak with him, and perhaps get an interview. I ran to the front entrance, only to see that there was nobody around. I stepped outside, looked up the street both ways, and spotted no one. On another occasion, while standing in the cellblock hallway in the basement, my associates and I were startled by the sound of metal hitting metal, similar to the closing of a cellblock door. There is only one metal door left in the prison, and that was about three feet in front of us, within our view. We searched for another door to no avail. We were not able to locate the origin of the noise and we were unable to recreate it with any debris that was in the basement area. The sense of being followed and the strong feeling of being watched were the most uncomfortable events we experienced that day. There is no doubt in my mind that the Black Jail of Guthrie, Oklahoma, could be one of the more haunted locations in this glorious historic town.

As the town continues to restore historic buildings to their original splendor, the prison is unfortunately one of the last to be attended to. A new roof was recently added to the structure to help eliminate any more damage from the elements. The town of Guthrie welcomes visitors and is in hopes of getting the Black Jail restored to its original state in the near future. Historical researchers, history buffs, and the town of Guthrie are anxiously awaiting the long past due renovation of the prison. Being so full of Western heritage, there is great hope that contributions will continue to pour in from historical foundations and individuals. If you would like to contribute to the prison's restoration efforts, please contact the Guthrie Chamber of Commerce.

VINA RAE'S GRILL & GRAZE

Avard, Oklahoma
By Tammy Wilson

The way Nan and I ended up meeting was rather strange. My sister had just recently moved to Cherokee, Oklahoma, which is not far from Avard. Her then-husband and his family were all from that area. I told them to keep their ears open for any stories of hauntings around there as I was always eager to hear new Oklahoma stories.

My sister called me one day to tell me she heard there was a haunted café in Avard. My first reaction (as is everyone else's I have encountered) was where the hell is Avard? She didn't know who owned the café or anything about it but she thought I should contact them. I said I would.

I didn't get a chance to find out much about it. My sister called me one Saturday morning a few weeks later and asked if I had called that lady in Avard yet. I assured her I would soon. That very day I received an email from Nan Wheatley, the owner of the café.

I assumed since all the towns around there are so small and everyone knows everyone that my sister or her husband's family had told her to contact me. That wasn't the case: she happened upon my website while looking for information about Oklahoma ghosts. There are several paranormal research groups in Oklahoma so it was strange that she happened to email me just when I had been planning on contacting her.

Nan asked if we would be interested in conducting an investigation at the café. I agreed that we would, so we set off to Avard, a tiny town in Woods County with a population of twenty-six in the 2000 census.

We arrived at the café and set up our equipment. I placed a meter that measures electrical and magnetic currents in an open doorway and went on to investigate the rest of the building. This particular meter was not a standard EMF detector; there are no buttons, just a dial that you turn it on with. Once it's set, it doesn't change and does not go off easily or randomly - except for this time. As I mentioned, it was placed in an open doorway. We were all in other areas of the building when we heard it going off. We returned to the area and there was nothing there and no one had entered or left through that door. I was not able to determine what caused it to go off, but that it did it so randomly was strange.

Nan went to get her business partner, Deb Campbell, and her mother,

Ramona Wheatley, who has since passed on. Ramon had sighed an apparition at the café. She told us about the time she was sitting in the café and saw a headless woman in a long gown, like the ones the ladies in the town used to wear for their lodge meetings, come right through the wall. It frightened her so badly that she was unable to sleep alone at her home for a few nights and would barely even set foot in the café after that incident. The reason Ramona was so credible was she was never a believer in the paranormal before this happened to her. She was an elderly woman and was highly respected in the town. In fact, she was the mayor at the time of our visit. We interviewed her and while she was telling us the story, Shirley McCoy, one of the team members from Eerie Oklahoma, took a picture and a huge orb appeared over our heads. Now, normally I don't put stock into orb photos, but this was odd because it was approximately where the apparition was said to have come out of the wall and it happened as Ramona was telling us her story! I examined the area and at first I thought it was a reflection from the lens of the video camera, but the camera was pointed down, not toward the wall at all. White paint often reflects camera flashes and this is likely what caused the orb, but the timing was indeed interesting.

Besides this sighting, Nan shared other things they have experienced at the café. Here's what she had to say:

"The odors are that of burning electrical wire or wood. Once it was pipe tobacco - a sweet tobacco, like cherry. Once it was cotton candy and the most sickening was hair. Burning hair. Not just a faint smell, but like someone's whole head had combusted. It was very over powering. The hair thing has happened more than once."

"Noises consist of knocks on the wall, footsteps, doors opening but really not, and voices. Mainly, the kitchen part is the only area where we've seen things move. The dish busboy rolled, broom handles have fallen over from a propped position, metal zipper pulls swayed. Just little things like that. Electrical problems such as tape recorders that won't record while

From left to right: Tammy Wilson interviewing Ramona Wheatley, as Alex Valliant and Deb Campbell listen. Nan Wheatley is in the foreground.

I'm gone and one of my salesmen's laptops would lose my orders and he says I'm the only place this ever happens."

"There have only been two actual encounters I know of, one of which being the woman coming at mom and something grabbed me by the shoulders years ago and threw me down the hall. Our dog goes to work with me and comes inside when he can, (not the café part). Anyway, his hair bristles up when he stares in certain spots and there are areas he won't go in and then there are times he will."

"The electricity has never been checked but the wiring is new. I climbed up above the ceiling several times when we noticed the smell but found nothing. This particular odor has only been associated with the hallway and by the French doors that open into the café . The smell is always located in about a three-by-three-foot square. Move out of that spot and the aroma is gone. Move back into that area and the smell is still there. Same way with the other smells. By the way, the burning hair was in the kitchen with me today. It was next to me for about two minutes and then gone. Just before that I heard a movement in front of me, about three feet away."

We conducted EVP (electronic voice phenomena) sessions in several areas of the building and we heard several knocking noises. Mike Valliant from Oklahoma Ghost Patrol stood at the doorways during most of them and listened from that standpoint. He also heard the noises and verified that there were no explainable reasons for them. Avard is a very small town and there were no people around but us. The EVP sessions were not conclusive.

There were some questionable pictures taken during our time at Vina Rae's. As I mentioned, I am not a fan of orb pictures by any means, but we did get some odd things. One photograph had a strange black mist that appeared as if it were hanging over our heads while we toured the kitchen. The light in the kitchen was very bright, so it did not make sense to us that there would be a shadowy spot in that area.

All in all, it was a relatively quiet evening, but that happens sometimes. I didn't discount the things that had been happening there, though, as I learned more about why they might be happening.

On March 13, 1956, a young woman named Mildred Ann Reynolds was burned to death in her car on a back road between Alva and Avard. An article in the February 1958 issue of *Real Detective* magazine, titled "Riddle of the Blazing Coed," tells the story of the unsolved mystery.

Reynolds was twenty-two and a senior at Northwestern State College in Alva (now Northwestern Oklahoma State University) when she met her untimely end. She was on her way home to Avard on an isolated country road when she was stopped by something - or someone - in the road. After that, no one really knows what happened, but a local wheat farmer noticed a column of black smoke billowing over the fields and hurried to investigate. Mildred and her car were found burning nearly beyond recognition out on that back road. The farmer hurried from the gristly scene to alert the sheriff.

When local law enforcement authorities arrived on the scene, they found the driver's side front door of the car open and Reynolds' body lying face-up across the front seat. One of her legs was burned completely away from the knee down and her arms were folded across her chest like those of a corpse in a coffin. Her head had been savagely beaten. There was damage to the front grill and the left fender of her 1949 Chevrolet Tudor sedan - likely the cause of a downed fence post and a mangled tree. Near the tree, investigators found patches of blood and one her loafers with blood on the toe. Reynolds' coat and scarf were lying discarded in the grass.

There were crazy tire tracks zigzagging down a nearby hill, which law enforcement officials believed were caused by Mildred encountering someone a the top of the hill and trying to turn the car around and get away. Had her car not hit the fence post and the tree, she might have succeeded. The clues indicate that she may have been taken out of the car and dragged into a nearby field, thus dislodging her shoe. Later, it appeared she was returned to the car and her body set on fire. While her body was too badly burned to discover whether she had been raped, an autopsy determined that she was still alive when she had been set ablaze. Tests were run with various accelerants to see what could have caused the car to burn from bumper to bumper so quickly and so thoroughly. The fire had been hot enough to melt the car's window glass.

Even with all the tests and theories, no one knows to this day exactly what happened to Mildred Ann Reynolds.

I'm certain at this point you're wondering how this might be related to Vina Rae's café. The café is located in the building that was once the Avard High School basketball gymnasium. Reynolds' husband of nine months was the basketball coach in the gym for a very long time and there is a theory that possibly Mildred is manifesting as the burning smell and returning to the place where she and/or her husband spent a lot of time. Perhaps she is looking for him.

Rumor has it around the town that some people knew who the killer was, but remained tight-lipped .

Strange things continue to happen at this small café in Avard, Oklahoma. Nan makes some of the best friend chicken and homemade gravy around, so if you're in the mood for some great home cookin' and a road trip, try Vina Rae's. You just might see a ghost - or smell one...

THE SKIRVIN HOTEL
Downtown Oklahoma City
By Tonya Hacker

One of Oklahoma's most puzzling haunts is the historic and beautiful Skirvin Hotel in downtown Oklahoma City. Packed full of history, the hotel, now the Skirvin Hilton Oklahoma City, is home to a handful of mysteries and of course, a scandal or two.

Built in 1910 by oilman William B. Skirvin, who was determined to create the most lavish hotel in the Southwest, the hotel opened first its doors in 1911. Guests were amazed at the Austrian crystal chandeliers, costing more than $100,000 each, the imported marble flooring, and the hand-carved woodwork in the lobby. Skirvin took pride in making a first-class impression and the hotel was soon the talk of the town. Going above and beyond was standard practice for Skirvin and it was proven to everyone who stayed at the fabulous hotel back in its early days. The Skirvin was the first hotel in the state to offer "iced air" within the then-244 room, ten-story structure. It was a welcomed amenity, especially to anyone who had experienced Oklahoma's scorching summer heat. The hotel was a hotspot for debutants, celebrities and politicians. Business was booming and money was flowing as people lived the high life in the Skirvin Hotel in the early 1900s.

With so many successful years of operation, its walls inevitably became packed full of happy memories and the occasional strange mishap. The Skirvin Hotel officially closed its doors in 1988. Looming and abandoned, the building sat dormant for 15 years on the corner of Park Avenue, adjacent to the Cox Convention Center.

During the last days of the hotel, one of the most popular ghost stories surfaced: the legend of Effie, said to be a former chambermaid who became W.B. Skirvin's mistress. W.B. is said to have tried to keep Effie's presence secret from the high-powered people he surrounded himself with. In time, the story goes, Effie became pregnant, an unacceptable condition for an unmarried woman in those days. The legend relates that W.B. agreed to give her free room and board on the hotel's tenth floor, as long as she agreed not to make their relationship public.

Shortly after the baby's birth, Effie became overwhelmed with postpartum depression. Her future must have seemed bleak - doomed to a life of shame, no money, no help and left to raise a child alone in secrecy.

A vintage postcard of the beautiful and historic Skirvin Hotel in downtown Oklahoma City.

When she could no longer contain her despair, she leaped to her death from the window of her tenth-floor room, with the illegitimate heir to the Skirvin empire clasped in her arms.

Or so the legend says.

As time went by, male guests staying alone at the hotel would be startled to hear a disembodied female voice propositioning them. Others have sworn they saw the insubstantial form of a nude woman join them while they were taking a shower. One man even claimed he was sexually assaulted by an invisible entity during his stay. Could this saucy spirit be Effie?

Historically, no documentation has been found about a woman fitting Effie's circumstances committing suicide at the hotel. Tracing through years of news articles and obituaries, her story is still unsubstantiated by researchers. Perhaps this is why the legend of Effie is one of the hotel's most puzzling hauntings. The inability to prove that Effie ever existed makes the case difficult to validate, but witness accounts hold a strong track record when it comes to ghostly phenomenon. Witnesses report seeing an apparition of a woman wearing a black calf-length skirt, red blouse, and high heels in the hallways of the tenth floor. Stiletto footsteps have been heard tapping high up in Skirvin's personal suite and wandering around the Venetian Room. The scent of perfume and a cold chill have been reported in the rooms of male guests traveling alone. The cry of an infant has also been reported descending from the east side of hotel, mostly on the upper floors. The story of Effie has lingered for years but to investigators, outside of a few outdated witness accounts, this legendary woman never existed and her scandalous affair never took place. But, as we all know, silence can be bought and in years gone by, newspapers could sometimes be persuaded not to report unfortunate events that could stain the reputations of prominent citizens.

Thirty years after the hotel's grand opening, parties and debutante balls were popular events. Outside of stylish facilities and alluring dining, the Skirvin Ballroom is remembered as a beautiful and spacious room, complete with polished parquet floors and the crafted elegance reminiscent of old Hollywood. Socialites were drawn to anything having to do with the majestic Skirvin.

All that was long past when I, along with several contemporaries, was granted permission to enter into the Skirvin Hotel to conduct a research assignment before the building was sold to the new owners. During our research we were able to conduct an experiment to see if we could validate some of our historical findings. We invited all types of different people from skeptics to believers to those who had no opinion at all to enter the hotel without telling them what our research had turned up. Allowing the participants to walk around the building with notebooks, walkie-talkies, and flashlights, we instructed them to only document what they saw, smelled, felt or heard. The experimental investigation lasted throughout the day and was followed up with a full investigation by local paranormal researchers that night.

What was reported from our volunteers helped us with validating rumors of a haunting with historical data we had collected. Most of the notebook entries were very brief and ranged from the sense of being watched to the sense of being followed up the main staircases but nothing alarming was documented. A few stronger impressions were acknowledged and we were taken aback somewhat when we compared the historical information we had collected with what was written in the notebooks. One of our volunteers is a professor of psychology at an Oklahoma City college. Being a self-proclaimed skeptic he had only one entry in his personal journal. He decided to investigate the hotel alone because he did not believe in such things as ghosts. In his notebook he had written, "I was touched on the shoulder in room 515." We did not share any of our historical findings with any of the volunteers. There was no way he would have known what we knew.

A few more notebooks were turned in and to our surprise there were several indications of strange occurrences and feelings of anxiety that took place in room 515. This was enough for us to declare that we may have discovered one of the hotel's spirits. About thirty years after the hotel's opening, we discovered that one of the managers met a strange and very sudden death. He was a well-known figure at the Skirvin, where he was one of the favorite event coordinators. We found a newspaper article reporting that the manager had coordinated a large debutante ball. Being the 1940s one could only imagine the delicate menu, rousing big band music, and glittering socialite guest list that was involved in the grand affair. The manager was reported to have walked out of the party and headed up to his room on the fifth floor where he then pulled out a handgun and blew his brains out beside his dresser. The newspaper reported his room number was 515 in the west wing of the hotel. We found it unusual that there was seemingly no reason why he ended his life so abruptly, without leaving a note.

This being such a seemingly pointless suicide, his death was a shock to everyone. He was an enthusiastic employee of the hotel and had put in many years of dedicated service. We were not able to find any more mention of the suicide in the papers beyond the initial story until a small article almost ten years later revealed that his death was a suspected murder and not suicide after all. Is the west wing of the fifth floor haunted by this dedicated employee? Historically speaking, we were able to validate the reasons why so many of our volunteers were experiencing such strange sensations on the fifth floor. Perhaps the former manager is waiting to see if anyone will ever take the time to uncover the truth behind his death. I am curious to see if the new operators of the hotel will begin to get strange reports coming from the fifth floor west wing.

On the second floor of the hotel, one can see more ornate architecture while peering down into the stunning lobby. If you take the grand west staircase to the second floor the first thing to meet your eyes is the entrance to the Pinstripe Bar. The bar has changed names a few times but has always returned to the handsome style of the Pinstripe. During Prohibition, the Pinstripe was the hotel's speakeasy where one could enjoy a martini and listen to the sounds of jazz favorites in a more intimate setting. Oklahoma oilmen and wealthy business owners deemed the Pinstripe to be worthy of their presence and of course, their money. During our research assignment we had one volunteer who was neither a skeptic nor a believer. He was a country boy who really had no opinion about the paranormal. He had also made the choice to investigate the hotel alone.

We heard him shouting and yelling profanities as if someone were attacking him - someone alive. When we arrived he was very anxious and unsure as to what had happened, but he insisted that somebody was in the Pinstripe Bar with him. We had our base camp set up in the lobby so we were confident that nobody had gotten past us and onto the second floor with him; we would have seen them. He related that as he entered the room, he walked towards the bar area and was startled by something behind him. It was as if someone had run right past him into the bar's kitchen. He immediately looked behind him, saw nothing, and assumed it had been a rat.

He said he approached the bar as would a customer and at that moment the room filled up with the smell of cigar smoke. He was excited, but mostly angry, which is a common reaction with nonbelievers. He said the smell was so strong he thought someone was in the room enjoying a cigar, but he did not see anyone nor did he see puffs of smoke. We all split up and looked for vagrants or anyone who could have sneaked into the hotel. We found no one who wasn't supposed to be there. Speaking further with the shaken man, it was clear he was upset about what had happened. He was ready to find the unseen smoker and literally beat him up! The smell of cigars was gone when we arrived and we asked him where it went. He was confused until it dawned on him that the strong smell had simply vanished. He was not able to explain who had run past him and of course could give no explanation for the cigar smell. At that point he literally looked as if he had seen a ghost. We were not able to find any history to validate this witness account, but we can say that with the colorful reputation of the Pinstripe and its clients, if walls could talk there would be no end to what we could learn about the state of Oklahoma.

Not all of the Skirvin's ghosts are inside the hotel. Back in the 1930s, it was no secret that real-life mafia members frequently visited Oklahoma City. The Skirvin Hotel was a very popular hangout for mobsters and high rollers, along with a few other places around town such as the Kentucky Club and Black Hotel. Sometimes things would get downright rough, from shootouts to kidnappings. One night in particular, for reasons unrevealed, gun-toting mobsters drove by the front doors of the hotel and opened fire. The identity of their target was unknown, but an innocent and well-loved doorman was caught in the crossfire and perished in the hotel entryway. According to a small article in the paper, the man died and nobody really seemed to pay much attention or try to find out whom the mobsters were gunning for. There have been a few reports of an African-American man in uniform walking to the front doors of the hotel only to vanish. Perhaps he is still there, a memory in time, in his coat, hat, and white gloves, helping guests with their bags, opening the door and occasionally smiling and being the very first to welcome you to the Skirvin Hotel in downtown Oklahoma City.

In our research we also found a newspaper article reporting that in the 1950s a traveling salesman checked into the Skirvin. He paid for his room in full and after receiving his room key from the front desk, he was seen hurriedly heading up the stairs to his eighth-floor suite. Apparently this man had other intentions than just enjoying a stay at the grand hotel. In a rush, he arrived from the main staircase to his rooms on the eighth floor, put down his bags, opened a window and jumped to his death. He landed in the courtyard on the north side of the building with parking attendants and passersby watching in horror as his body splattered onto the pavement. He did not leave a suicide note and the papers reported that he had no immediate family. According to his belongings, he was not making his desired quota in sales.

Reports of experiencing a feeling of being followed while walking up the main staircase were very common during our experiments. I personally experienced this as I felt as if an unseen force was trying to hurry me up the stairs. It was uncomfortable feeling, as if someone was behind me as I climbed several flights of stairs, enough to make me stop and allow whoever was there to pass by. There were no more mentions of the salesman in the newspapers beyond the initial article. To date, this case is without confirmation and is a possible validation to some supernatural occurrences on the staircase. In our research, nobody reported the sense of being rushed on any of the other stairs past the eighth floor.

The hopes of this paranormal historian are for future eyewitness accounts. Now that the hotel has reopened, the legends of the past may become better known. Contractors and workers hired to take part in the Skirvin's $46.4 million-dollar restoration have spoken about their ghostly encounters while on the job. A chance meeting of an old high school friend brought out some new stories about some of the hotel's haunting legends. While working to remove asbestos prior to the hotel's re-opening, my friend told me about the pranks that most of the men automatically assumed were played by each other. Misplaced tools and the feeling of someone tugging on coveralls while the wearers were balanced atop ladders were enormously common.

My friend told me a story of how he had officially met one of the inhabitants of the fourth floor one gloomy Oklahoma afternoon. Arriving at the hotel, he headed up to his work area where he was instructed to begin work on the east side of the fourth floor. There were other workers moving about but he insisted that no one was in his particular area. Covered head to toe in his protective clothing, he began to drill holes as if it were just another day until he experienced something that he could not explain. As he worked, he peered down to the north end of the hallway where he noticed what appeared to be a man in a tailored suit. He was curious because the man did not have on any asbestos protection gear. He turned away to shut down his equipment and when he looked back, the man was gone. He was startled but more confused as to who the man was. He thought it was one of the owners or someone official tied to the hotel. He walked into the main hallway but nobody was around who fit the description of the man he had just seen. He headed to the west wing to ask a buddy if he had seen anyone in a suit and of course, nobody else had seen him. While interviewing him I asked him what kind of suit it was, to see if I could put a date on this strange apparition, and he told me it was a standard suit similar to ones men wear today. I asked if there was anything else that could possibly help identify the man and he told me there was no hat or anything that stood out. "He looked like a regular businessman, nothing extraordinary at all."

After being slightly spooked he went back to work. Other reports of odd events started materializing as the jokes about him seeing a ghost started to circulate amongst the workers. Stories included tools being moved out of reach and sometimes just vanishing altogether. My friend jokingly told me, "Somewhere in the hotel are a lot of tools hidden in the walls or something. If you ever find them, call me up."

He remembered a lot of the workers complaining that vagrants were getting into the building and stealing tools, but nobody ever even saw the mysterious tool thieves, much less caught them in the act. To date he is still mystified by who the man in the suit was. He has come to the conclusion that it may have indeed been a ghost, but he wondered why the ghost was watching him work. The concept that it was Skirvin, the hotel's original owner, makes sense to many, but his identity is still up in the air. I emailed my friend a photo of W.B. Skirvin and he stated, "It is not him; it was another man."

With the hotel's eclectic history and the lack of identification of any of the apparitions that have been seen there, the haunting history of the Skirvin seems to be such a large assignment that most paranormal historians would hesitate to tackle it. As much as I love and respect the hotel, it is an assignment I would be happy to take on.

Politicians and socialites were common clients of the Skirvin. Fundraisers, political celebrations, weddings and debutante socials, conventions and gatherings of "who's who" in Oklahoma were the highlight of its nearly 80 years in operation. Big bands roared in the elaborate Venetian Room high atop the fourteenth floor. Memories of money, fame and, of course, society's dirty little secrets that were discussed only between its walls abound. Family scandals broke loose during the later years of the hotel's history. Even W.B's own daughter filed a lawsuit against her father because of money issues. Pearle Mesta, a very familiar name in Oklahoma, was said to want more from the elaborate life her father provided her as she grew up in the hotel. Pearle grew into a famous socialite in Oklahoma, across the Midwest, and eventually in Washington, D.C., where she became known as "the hostess with the mostess." She single-handedly brought the hotel to national headlines as she became the American ambassador to Luxembourg. The Broadway musical "Call Me Madam" was based on her exploits. Perle's personal connections allowed her to bring in more money and important people to Oklahoma. The guest list at the sophisticated parties she hosted at the Skirvin included celebrities, royalty, politicians and wealthy businessmen from across the nation. She would not hold back when it came to accommodating anyone who was willing to pay to stay at the hotel. Her father appreciated and supported his daughter at this time because it was good for business and the hotel.

To indicate how far Pearle and W.B. would go to please their guests, when a very well-known circus owner visited Oklahoma City for a weekend, they rented out two rooms for his famous tamed tigers. There was no end to the hotel's charm and this is why it is such a rich part of Oklahoma history. The over-indulgence in luxury eventually led to the grand hotel closing its doors. The Skirvin name had been picked away as the bills piled up. The only things left were decades of wonderful memories of grand events. Once a millionaire with grandiose dreams, W. B. Skirvin eventually died of old age in his very humble home, leaving an estate estimated to be worth less than forty thousand dollars. W.B. led a good life only to have his dreams crushed by greed, power and unmet liabilities.

Some say that William Skirvin still walks the halls of the grand hotel. There is no proof of this of course, but what folks hold dear in their hearts is the fact that he made the hotel what it is today. The rebirth of the hotel holds a lot of forgotten memories to be unfolded as people rediscover the past and the dedication W.B. had to strive for the best as the dirt road state of Oklahoma gave way to the paved streets and the monumental legacy of the Skirvin Hotel that was part of the birth of the booming metropolis of Oklahoma City. The hotel helped form friendships with out-of-state business owners who were shown that Oklahoma was soon to be a city that could compete with Dallas, Chicago, and even New York. Upon opening its doors, the hotel became a one-stop networking connection that later helped develop some of the larger downtown corporations that are still in business today. Opening the doors to the motion picture business, the hotel housed celebrities and film agents from across the nation, assisting with the development of Oklahoma City's historic Film Row. Skirvin also allowed the city's first radio station, now known as WKY Radio, to hit the airwaves. Easy listening, big band music and the local news were all broadcast from the hotel.

Now that the historic Skirvin Hotel has a new face and its charm is restored, I would like to invite you to spend the night in there. Refurbished to its original grandeur, I guarantee you will find yourself thrown back in time as you experience the hotel for yourself. Don't be surprised if you hear the swinging sound of a big band orchestra in the air as you relax in your private chambers. Just enjoy it and recognize it as a privileged glimpse into yesterday. As you enter the lobby, don't forget about the doorman who once greeted guests with a smile as bright as the sun. If you're a gentleman lodging alone, and you are awakened by the sweet breath or scent of a woman, don't fret, she is just seeking your love and affection; she will be gone soon. If you take a walk inside the hotel do not be amazed if you smile and tip your hat to someone who is not there. Your subconscious is paying attention, even if you are preoccupied. If you dare to be adventurous and rent the room closest to the original room 515 and you are tapped on the shoulder or startled in any way, just remember that whoever it is just wants you to remember him and understand that his life was not in vain. If you do come across any of the ghosts of the Skirvin, don't be afraid, simply say thank you and remind them that they are not forgotten.

FROM DADDY

When Daddy was alive he collected coins, not as a serious collector, but he would always have small piles of them around. After he passed we found several small boxes full of coins.

About a month after Daddy died I started finding dimes. They would be in really obscure places. If I was thinking about daddy or having a particularly tough time suddenly a dime would appear.

I would "find" dimes often. After sweeping and moping, I turned around to discover three dimes in the middle of the floor. I would get up in the morning and put on my shoes to find a dime in each of them, or open a book and there in the crease of my page would be a dime. I would move something in order to dust under it and there would be a dime right in the middle of where the object had been sitting. Once, I was drinking a glass of tea and when I picked it up to take another sip, there was a dime under my glass. Never a quarter, a penny or a nickel, and each time something told me it was from Daddy.

At first it would bring tears to my eyes but now I find them comforting. I just know they are telling me that even though Daddy has been gone nearly seven years, he wants me to know he is still here with me.

At present I have one hundred and eighty-four dimes in my jewelry box. I know Daddy will continue to bring these gifts of his, just because...

CLAY HALL

By Tammy Wilson

Anyone who has lived in Enid, Oklahoma, for any amount of time is probably familiar with a buff-colored brick building called Clay Hall, the old women's dorm of the former Phillips University. Northern Oklahoma College now owns the campus and the building. I attended Phillips in 1991 and 1992 and Clay Hall was closed then. Over the years, the windows have been broken and have since become boarded up. The building is condemned and off-limits.

Clay Hall sits atop a hill on the south side of the campus, all alone and somehow ominous-looking, separated from the rest of the campus by an expanse of lawn and a lake with a narrow bridge. Like with most big empty buildings, it has become a little foreboding and stories have circulated about its demise. Some are based in truth and some are simply far-fetched and silly, made up to make your friends jumpy on a dark night of snooping where you shouldn't be.

There are stories of girls being attacked in Clay Hall and at least one story about a girl committing suicide there. I have not verified the suicide story. I have, however, verified stories of attacks, but I am not certain if the attacker was a janitor, as some of the folk legends insist. One of my favorite tall tales is that somewhere on the adjacent golf course there exists a "Gateway to Hell." Perhaps the fact that Clay Hall sits atop the hill all alone is why it seems so spooky, but the golf course is a regular run-of-the-mill golf course, not a gateway to eternal damnation, as far as I can tell, unless you consider your years in college to be less than favorable.

The building opened in 1946. It was closed down in the early 1980s because it was a fire hazard. Its layout is quite odd. You go into a room you think is off the hall and realize there is a doorway there to another hall on the other side of the wall. It would indeed be hard to get people out quickly in an emergency. I believe there were also some asbestos issues as well. They haven't destroyed it because it would be a very costly undertaking and there has been talk of using it every now and then, but I don't think they ever will. When I spoke to someone at the college, they explained there was a lot of water damage inside and it was quite a mess. I contacted one of the former Phillips librarians and after both of us doing research we came up pretty empty-handed when it came to a real reason for the building to be haunted. That's not say people haven't had unexplained experiences there, however.

A former classmate of mine, Ricardo Padilla, recounts what happened to him:

"I had always heard stories about Clay Hall. I never really wanted to believe them because, first, I was a skeptic, and second, I never believed a drunk. I spent much of my time around Clay Hall under the influence. Be that as it may, my skepticism rarely wavered. There are two occurrences that stand out in my mind.

I remember being in Clay Hall one time and hearing about a girl who had committed suicide in one of the rooms. Never one to believe mumbo jumbo, I joined a group of adventurers and wandered aimlessly through the practically condemned building. We happened to enter a room where the suicide supposedly happened. It was a room I believed to be facing south. The windows looked toward a certain section of our school golf course. It was noticeably colder in this room. I just thought through the power of suggestion maybe I only believed it was cooler. Nonetheless, I was quick to hurry out of the room.

Shortly after that, I had the opportunity to reenter the building, but I didn't. I was hanging out with a fellow student and declined to enter the off-limits property. I was then interrogated by security and the Enid police because an alarm was tripped. I was definitely hopping mad about this one. Apparently, I appeared to have been the distraction the others needed while they actually broke in.

The second time I experienced weirdness involving Clay Hall, I was walking home from a house party. I was alone. I happened to look up and saw a figure looking at me from about the same area where I had previously been: the room that allegedly housed the suicide victim. I didn't believe my eyes at first, so I glanced again. It almost seemed as if I could make out a girl with long hair with a strange glow and eyes that followed me. I knew this was impossible. There was no way I could see any features, especially eyes, at the distance I was. But I did. So, I did what most people I know would do: I freaked out and started sprinting toward the dorms as fast as I could. Still, to this day, I occasionally dream about this place. It spooks me and I'm not usually spooked."

So, is Clay Hall really haunted? Or are spirits of another kind taking their toll on college students and causing them to have overactive imaginations? Perhaps the lights people reported seeing back in the early nineties were kids playing and exploring the vacant, looming building. Whatever the explanation, it is definitely a foreboding building and we had our share of being completely spooked while playing hide and seek in there back in the day. Even now when I drive by, it gives me goose bumps. I think it was more than imaginations.

THE LITTLE LOST GIRL
By Elizabeth S. Tyree

There are stories of hauntings everywhere: old houses, hotels, graveyards, even entire towns are purported to be haunted. How, why and by whom they are haunted; however, can often become lost in the translation by teenagers and adults alike, trying to scare themselves up some fun. This is the case at many reportedly haunted sites here in Alva, Oklahoma.

For example, there have been many reported hauntings in Alva's Hatfield Park. How do we know which ones are true and which are a hoax? One way is to experience them for yourself. This is exactly what I did, although I didn't mean to at the time.

One night, a few years ago, I was feeling particularly claustrophobic in my little house and, wanting to put off writing a paper, I decided to go spend some time in the great outdoors; namely in the field near Hatfield Park's hiking trails. As I was sitting at a picnic table, reading and relaxing in the cool night air, I heard a young girl's voice. Although I was in a park, I found it a little curious that there was such a young-sounding child there after dark. I began wondering where her parents were.

As I looked around for the source of the voice, I saw a young girl, about six or seven years old, standing near an old tree at the far edge of the field. She was alone and wearing an old-fashioned white dress, although not so old-fashioned that it registered immediately. Although she seemed a little pale, it didn't occur to me that she was a ghost until after I tried to talk to her.

When I asked her where her parents were, she merely looked away. After a little while waiting for her to answer, I asked again where her where her parents were. This time, she looked at me and said her father was a bad man, that he hurt her. I told her we could get help, but she said she didn't need help anymore and just wanted to be left alone, that her mother was coming and wouldn't like it if she was talking to strangers. I agreed and turned to walk back to my seat, when I looked back, she was gone. At first I thought I was imagining things, or that my blood sugar had gotten too low again, but then my friends called me a few nights later, saying that they thought they had heard a little girl's voice in the park, calling out to her mother. They couldn't find the girl and thought it was their imaginations. I hadn't told them about my encounter and it was only after I heard heir story that I realized I had not been hallucinating.

I've had several other encounters with the little ghost girl over the past few years. Over time I have learned that she was abused and ultimately killed by her father, although I believe him to be a step-father, because she talks lovingly of daddy, a man who "went away" when she was four. She was buried by this "father" somewhere in the area, and she returns to the park to wait for her mother to find her. She still refuses to tell me her name; her mother doesn't like her talking to strangers, and she doesn't know her parent's names, except that they are mommy and dad. She has, however, told me that she doesn't like the changes that have been made to the park over the years. Hatfield used to have a zoo with a "monkey" (Charlie the Baboon), deer, ducks, etc. and she is very upset that the zoo has disappeared, along with most of the pond. She does like it when people bring their dogs to walk the trails, although she is upset that she can't play with them. Most dogs strain to get away from her, which she doesn't understand. The little girl has also introduced me to the spirit of a nice older gentleman, who she calls grandpa, who wanders down from the nearby cemetery every once in a while. While I still don't know her name, I feel somehow connected to this sweet little girl whose spirit waits patiently day after day for her mother to find her.

JUST A DREAM?

Submitted by Beth Reaves

My family moved to Davis, Oklahoma, during our school's Christmas break in 1967. My father was to become the new pastor of the First Christian Church there. From the time I was seven until I was thirteen we lived in the parsonage next door to the church.

When I was about thirteen, my mom and dad, my three brothers, baby sister and I all moved down the street into a two-story brick house that had been built in the 1930s. The same family that had built that house had built a previous house on the same lot: a two-story white frame Victorian with a wrap-around porch. After demolishing the old frame house, the family made use of some of the French doors, light fixtures, and bathroom fixtures from the old house in their new, more modern, brick home. Before we moved in, the house needed painting and some other repairs. My family and some friends from our church did the work.

While working on the house one day in preparation of our move, a bad storm was brewing on the west side of town. The tornado siren blew. My family and some of our neighbors took shelter in the basement of the old house. The grown-ups were all talking to each other on one side of the large basement, and us kids were gathered in another corner chattering with excitement about the possibility of being hit by the oncoming tornado. One of us, I don't remember who, first heard footsteps overhead coming from the living room and walking toward the kitchen. We all stopped talking and listened intently. The footsteps sounded like they stopped on the tile floor of the kitchen, directly overhead. We broke in on our parents' conversation and reported what we'd heard. My dad quickly climbed the basement stairs to investigate. But he could find no one anywhere in the house, and the doors were locked. That was the first thing I remember being involved with something that seemed uncanny.

During the preparation of the new parsonage, one of my friends who'd volunteered from church was in the house alone, vacuuming the bedroom carpets upstairs. She heard what sounded like a door shutting, so she turned off the vacuum cleaner. Listening intently, she heard the swinging door from the hallway downstairs that led to the stairway swing open, then close again, and footsteps coming up the stairs. Those stairs had a turn in them, and from where she was standing she would not be able to see who was there until they reached the top of the stairs. Expecting to see one of my family, or another church volunteer approaching, she stood still and watched. When the sound of the footsteps reached the top of the stairs, there was no body there to have produced them. It frightened her, but like so many people do when such a thing occurs, she decided to ignore it. She turned the vacuum cleaner back on and hurriedly continued working. Once she'd finished her job, she made a hasty exit, and made certain to never be in the house alone again.

After moving in we often heard water turn on upstairs when we were all downstairs, but when we went up to see who'd done it, someone or something had turned the water off before we arrived. Likewise, we heard water turn on in the downstairs bathroom when we were upstairs   and once again, something would turn it off before we were able to get there. We all heard the bodiless footsteps that came up the stairs and stopped at the top of the stairway.

One night I was preparing for bed. I had closed my door, turned out the light, and pulled the covers up under my chin. I began hearing things moving around on my bookcase across the room. I jumped up and turned on the light only to have the noises cease abruptly. Upon close inspection, I saw nothing unusual and nothing was out of place. I once again turned out the light, got back in bed, and almost immediately the scuffling noises resumed on my bookcase. That was enough for me! I jumped up and ran out of the room and into the den where my mother was watching television. I described to her what had happened, and she explained it away by saying I probably had a mouse in my room. She went in my room to see if she could find the "mouse" for me, but she, too, could find nothing. She tried to soothe me, and talked me into going back to bed. This time, when I turned out the light and got in bed, something much more frightening began: I heard what sounded like a fingernail scraping from the bottom of my bedspread slowly, slowly, all the way up until it was directly under my chin! My heart was pounding so hard I could hear it in my ears, and I could hardly breathe, I was so scared! But I didn't make a sound, in hopes that if I pretended not to hear it, if I just didn't react to it, it would go away. It then very sloooowly scraped down to the foot of my bed where it had begun and stopped. I can't explain how I did it, but I just lay there listening, until I finally, and thankfully, fell asleep.

Another night, I was awakened by the sound of knocking coming from behind my headboard. It continued for a bit. There was no room on the other side of the wall, so there was no way a person could have been knocking. And no, there was no plumbing in that wall.

One whole wall of my upstairs bedroom was covered in windows. I loved it. There was a pecan tree right outside my bedroom, and one Saturday morning after awakening, I was leisurely lying on my side in bed, gazing outside at some birds that were perched in the tree. I felt someone sit on the edge of my bed, and then get up. I assumed it was my little brother, because he would crawl in bed with me sometimes in the morning. I said something like, "If you're getting in, just get in," and turned over. To my surprise, I saw a little boy with a blonde burr haircut, wearing blue jean cut-off shorts and a white t-shirt. It wasn't my little brother. He was standing there quietly looking out my window. He looked like a flesh and blood person, except I could see the faint outline of objects on the other side of the room through his body. I very quickly turned back towards the window. I was petrified with fear! My heart was pounding inside my chest. Then I felt someone get on the bed behind me again, as the blanket pulled tight around my shoulders. It felt as if someone was on his knees behind me, leaning and reaching over my body while resting his weight on his hand on the bed right in front of me. BUT NOBODY WAS THERE!

I jumped up as quickly as I could and raced downstairs to the kitchen where my mother was cooking bacon for Saturday breakfast. I must have looked as if I'd seen a ghost or something, which I had, because she asked me, "What's wrong?" I told her what had occurred. She tried to convince me that I had been dreaming. I was certain I had been fully awake, and told her so. She said she knew I believed I was awake, but that I must have been asleep. That was the only plausible explanation.

One night, my older brother Mark was sleeping in the basement. My oldest brother Donnie had made the basement his makeshift bedroom, basically so he'd have a private place to "crash" when he came in late when visiting from college. Mark had decided to sleep down there one Friday night so my parents wouldn't catch him coming in late. The next morning he woke me up in my room, asking if I had come down into the basement and slept with him the night before. It was obvious to me that he was really shaken up. I told him I had been in my room all night. He then rushed into my little brother Steven's room, woke him up, and asked him the same thing. Steven said he'd been in his own bed all night, as well. With an ashen face, Mark told us that in the middle of the night he woke up and felt someone in bed with him. He couldn't see because it was too dark, so he reached over and felt beside him, and found a very thin arm. He said for some reason the did not think it was a flesh and blood person, but he was too afraid to find out for sure, so he just lay there until he finally fell back asleep. When he woke up in the morning, no one was in bed with him, and that was when he came upstairs to ask if it was either of us.

Then there was the night my brother Donnie was driving Mark and me home, Donnie told us about something that had happened to him in the basement. When he would be sleeping down there, he would leave the door to the first floor open and leave a light on in the hallway so he could see to get to the bathroom, if needed. He said he woke up and felt someone watching him. He looked over by the stairs and could see a woman standing there, wearing a long, late 1800s dress, with a bonnet on her head. He said she was greenish in color, and smoky, but he could clearly see her, although he could not see any distinguishable facial features. He said he was so scared he shouted out, "WHAT DO YOU WANT? WHY ARE YOU BOTHERING ME? GO AWAY!" (Or something to that effect.) He said she then vanished. I asked him when it had happened, and why he'd never told me before. He said it had happened a few months before, maybe three or four, and he didn't like to talk about it. We then all realized that in the last three or four months none of us had heard anything unusual, or had anything odd happen. And nothing else did, that I'm aware of, all the way up until the time we moved. I wondered if when my brother shouted at the apparition and asked her to leave him alone she went ahead and "crossed over."

I had the opportunity to speak with Ms. Wolfe, a woman in her late eighties, who was a relative of the Wolfe family who'd built both the original white frame house that had stood on that lot, as well as the brick house that we lived in. I asked her if anyone had ever died in either of the houses. She said not that she could remember, but that in the first house there had been a daughter who was ill and quite frail. She couldn't remember what the daughter's infirmity was, but she'd died in a carriage on the way to see a doctor, if she remembered correctly. The daughter was twenty-one or so when she died. I asked about any little boys but she didn't remember any boys dying. However, the boys who'd lived there before my family, Doug and Joe Don, were killed in a car wreck along with their mother shortly after they moved away from Davis. Maybe the little boy I saw was Joe Don. His hair was blonde, and he wore it in a burr-style cut.

Back when these things happened I was absolutely certain of everything I've told you. But time has a way of making us doubt our memories. Over the years I've wondered if maybe I did not see a little boy at all. I wore contacts back then for near-sightedness. When I woke up that morning I did not have them in and did not have my glasses on. Maybe I saw something else in the room that just looked like a little boy. And maybe my mother was right. Maybe I dreamed it all.

But I don't think so...

A HAUNTING IN HUGO

By Tonya Hacker

I have to admit, when I was assigned to locate haunted bed and breakfasts in Oklahoma and parts of Texas I was ecstatic! With my love for the paranormal for and self-indulgent places where I can rest my weary head and take hot bubble baths, I soon realized that my assignment just rocked!

The first project given to us with *O.P.E.N. Magazine* was to head to southern Oklahoma, territory that I will admit scared the bejesus out of me. Once we arrived I realized that Hugo, Oklahoma, had a lot more to offer than just a local Wal-Mart. Entering Hugo, it looked like a regular small town in southern Oklahoma, but what was behind that typical shell of a town was some great ghostly tales that Hugonians love to share with tourists.

We had previously made lodging arrangements, and I will swear that nobody had any prior knowledge of the ghost stories attached to this particular B & B; and believe me, we looked for a haunted one! Arriving at the Old Johnson House Inn, I noticed a familiar sense, as if I had been there before. Heading up the steps of the porch, I suddenly realized that the Old Johnson House was very similar to another infamous bed and breakfast in Guthrie, Oklahoma, that I have had the opportunity to visit and investigate as a ghost hunter. I moved closer to the front door and that familiar sense of something unknown grew stronger. As we walked across the wrap-around porch toward the front door, we were warmly welcomed by the innkeeper, Metra Christofferson, and her pug, Oliver Edwin Twist, a.k.a. Ollie.

Heading in, I couldn't resist exclaiming, "You gotta tell me the ghost story about this place, it is just amazing!" There was no doubt in my mind that the Old Johnson House held a secret or two. Metra started to explain a little about the house and smiled mischievously as she led us into the living room.

Built in 1910, this Victorian beauty was the home of the Johnson Family up until the mid-1980s. Since being converted into a bed and breakfast, some say that Mrs. Johnson still lingers the halls. My eyebrow rose, I'm sure of it.

While I sat, listening like a little kid during story time, Metra related the inn's history. She said Judge Johnson built the home for his wife and adult children. It is believed that Johnson was one of the last "hanging judges" in

The Old Johnson House Inn in Hugo, Oklahoma

Oklahoma Territory.

The house was Mrs. Johnson's dream home where she kept a close eye on her family. It is not definite how many adult children lived with the Johnsons, but it is certain there were no fewer than three.

One of the Johnson children was Edgar Allen. Edgar moved into the home upon its completion in 1910. He became a doctor of obstetrics after the birth of his first and only child, which ended in the tragic deaths of both child and mother. The grieving young widower never remarried. He graduated from medical school and sat up his practice in Hugo, vowing to save the lives of future mothers and their unborn children.

It is said that Edgar Johnson's mother kept a firm grasp on her family even when they were adults. Her husband's judicial past as a hanging judge was not one to be proud of and rumor has it that is why his wife tried hard to be a prominent and good citizen of Hugo.

When the current owner, Metra Christofferson, purchased the home, she was approached several times from strangers walking by who continued to ask her, "Have you met Mrs. Johnson yet?" She was puzzled, but stated that she does not easily succumb to the power of suggestion. As she continued on with her minor renovations, Metra was frequently approached by locals who told her about unexplained goings-on in her house, about footsteps being heard on the staircase, shadows glimpsed in the mirrors, Mrs. Johnson's rocking chair gently moving back and forth when no one was sitting in it and curtains moving when there was no breeze blowing. Metra was perplexed as to why she had not experienced such things while she

spent so much time alone in the house. Speaking further with Metra we discovered that she is extremely comfortable in the house. Could that be why she has not experienced anything unusual?

A former housekeeper at the Inn contacted Metra one day with the intention of finding out if she had yet witnessed the ghost of Mrs. Johnson walking to her room on the first floor. The former housekeeper insisted that Mrs. Johnson was still in the home, "just there, being Mrs. Johnson." She said eerie occurrences took place during her time working at the inn. Metra still awaits this type of proof, but she leaves it up to her guests to report any strange phenomenon.

Having stayed at the inn, I will have to admit that some parts of the house seem to have a slight personality, but nothing scary and nothing malicious, just a sense of being watched and that warm tingling sensation that I actually kind of enjoyed.

Mrs. Johnson's portrait still hangs in the main hallway heading to her former bedroom, now called the Red Room. The setting is just like it was many years ago; in fact, there are some of the original Johnson furnishings throughout the house. Mrs. Johnson's favorite rocking chair still faces toward the windows in the Red Room. Many things are left untouched in the Old Johnson House, and that is how Metra wants to keep it.

During renovations many hidden items were discovered, including toddler-sized nightgowns packed inside the walls. To this day the nightgown discovery is still a mystery. Nobody is sure to whom the gowns belonged. Small children were not known to have been part of the Johnson family.

Outside of the Old Johnson House Inn being one of the cleanest bed and breakfasts I have ever stayed in, I have to give this trip rave reviews for the simple fact that Metra made homemade marshmallows! I have never thought once about the actual origin of marshmallows. I had to ask, who the hell makes homemade marshmallows? To me that was beyond paranormal! As she served us hot chocolate with marshmallows with little hearts cut out of them, I realized that this was not your run of the mill B&B. This place had real charm, a very rare thing to find these days even in the most upscale B&B's across the Midwest.

During our visit to the Old Johnson House Inn I personally did not witness anything that I would declare remarkably paranormal. But, like I mentioned, there are parts of the house that seemed to have a personality of their own. I ran my tape recorder in an attempt to catch the voice of Mrs. Johnson but I had no luck this time around. I snapped a few photos and nothing vaporous showed up. But I want to report that while relaxing in my bubble bath I did hear what to me sounded like someone whisper in my ear. I was alone and the air in the bathroom seemed to have shifted, as if someone entered. It was not a daunting feeling, just a feeling as if your grandma came in to check on you to see if you were okay in the tub.

While spending time in the Red Room, I stood alone and stared at the rocking chair. For some reason, I couldn't make myself sit in it. I felt it was not my place and I also felt that if I did, I would sit on someone. It is never polite to sit on someone's lap without permission. The Red Room had a strange sense to it, as if it were someone's personal space. The feeling of not being alone was strong but comforting.

Perhaps the ghost of Mrs. Johnson still lingers in the halls of her dream home. Her family lived with her up until her death; maybe she just could never find the strength to leave a place that holds so many memories. Whatever the circumstances may be, the ghost of Mrs. Johnson is not going away and she is welcomed and highly recognizable to the locals.

The innkeeper of the Johnson House invites all of her guests to visit and enjoy what she has to offer. Journals are a new thing at the Johnson house and are placed in each and every room. Ms. Christofferson invites everyone to document their ghostly experiences and to read previous entries. If nothing strange happens at least leave a comment on how you enjoyed your stay.

The Old Johnson House Inn is located at 1101 E. Kirk St., Hugo, Oklahoma, 74743, (580) 326-8111. Or you can email for reservations at **metra@oldjohnsonhouse.com**. The inn is available for multi-day meetings and private weekend retreats and will soon host murder mystery dinners.

Attention Ghost Hunters: The innkeeper does not mind teams coming in for paranormal investigations or research, but keep in mind she is running a business. Business at most B&Bs is slow during the week and if you rent your rooms during those times there is a better chance of having the use of the inn without other guests being present. Metra invites teams to come and investigate, but she is unable to allow anyone in for free in exchange for online advertising. Experience the B&B for what it is, and wake up to fresh coffee and a fabulous breakfast after your investigation.

One more thing: the majority of paranormal experiences happen to guests, not to paranormal investigative teams. Perhaps Mrs. Johnson has something to do with that.

No matter if you are visiting the Old Johnson House as a guest or a paranormal fan, you are sure to be satisfied with your stay.

THE UNEARTHING OF SOMETHING WEIRD IN THE BEAVER SANDS
(THE TRUE STORY OF THE BEAVER SANDS PORTAL, ALSO KNOWN AS THE SHAMAN'S PORTAL)
By Tammy Wilson

Besides researching purportedly haunted places, we also research urban legends and local folklore. I ran across one story that was particularly intriguing to me: the Beaver Sands Portal, or Shaman's Portal, as some call it. It is supposedly a "portal" in the sand dunes in Beaver, Oklahoma, where several people have disappeared, much like the Bermuda Triangle. There are several theories about the portal, one of the most popular being that it is a UFO crash site. When I heard about this place, I immediately began planning a trip and doing as much research as I could on it. The following is what I found out and my account of what happened when I looked too far into something so weird...

Richard E. Bohlander, editor of World Explorers and Discoverers, 1992, The *Journey of Coronado*, tells the history of the portal.

Francisco Vasquez de Coronado was born in Salamanca, Spain in 1510. When he was 25, he set sail for the new world and eventually settled in what is now Mexico City. He raised a family there and in 1538 he was appointed governor of the province of Nueva Galicia.

There were reportedly riches in the fabled Seven Cities of Cibola and in 1540 Coronado led an expedition of nearly one thousand men into what is now the Southwestern part of the United States and northern Texas. Much of the party returned to Mexico the following year after being unsuccessful at finding any gold, but Coronado and a smaller group charged ahead only to return to Mexico in 1542 empty-handed.

Even though the disastrous expedition caused Coronado to lose some credibility, he returned to his post as councilman and remained there until his death in 1554.

Coronado may not have returned with any gold, but the expedition did fuel many stories of lost treasures buried in Texas and what has long been called No Man's Land in the panhandle of Oklahoma. Some of these tales were documented while others were passed down by word of mouth. One particular legend emerged from the others and remained a mystery for quite some time: that of the Shaman's Portal, or the Beaver Sands Portal. The

Shaman's Portal is said to be nestled in the sand dunes near Beaver, Oklahoma, in Beaver State Park. The Native Americans were aware of this portal, or gateway, into the unknown and Coronado and his men experienced it as well. A friar who accompanied Coronado's expedition logged the occurrence in his journal: "It was the work of El Diablo. That night by the sandy hills we had been warned by the natives to avoid, we lost three able-bodied men of valour: Juan Viscaino, Marco Romano, and Juan Munoz. They had been hunting game for the men when the three ill-fated men were taken from us in a lightening bolt of green." (Translated by Albert Gettis, The Journal Discourses of Fray Juan de Padilla, 1543)

Apparently, another soldier on the expedition also recorded the incident but was ordered by Coronado to strike it from the log. It took centuries for the truth to come out. In 1993, bits and pieces of the truth began to surface. There had been disappearances in the area up until 1987 and each one was documented as being accompanied by a flash of green light. Was this why the natives called it No Man's Land?

With each new generation, explorers set out to find the answer to that question; the most recent being an investigator by the name of Dr. Mark Thatcher. Thatcher reported that he researched the area for three years after receiving reports from an Oklahoma State University archaeologist. In 1995, he hired a geologist to test the location and they found samplings of ionized soil cores. There was also a great deal of electromagnetic interference in the area. There were many similarities between the Beaver Sands Portal, the Bermuda Triangle, and the Roswell crash site. The team was discovered during their research and warned off by men in suits who produced very official-looking government credentials. Their careers were threatened if they were to ever return to the site or to speak publicly about it.

Because of the incident with the possible men in black in the middle of Beaver State Park, Thatcher was led to believe that rather than a portal into the unknown, they were possibly dealing with a UFO crash site. Thatcher explained that the ionized soil cores, the green light, and the disappearances might all be explained by the fact that there was a spacecraft buried beneath the sand dunes of Oklahoma with some of its elements still intact and working. He left the site and was planning to return when yet another odd occurrence took place.

A man and his family were camping at Beaver Sands during a family reunion when they witnessed military-looking people excavating what can only be described as a spacecraft from beneath the dunes under cover of darkness. The family was detained by these officials for over three hours and threatened in various ways, only to be released some ten miles from where they had been camping and forced to return to their campsite on foot. They maintained their silence for years, finally decided to share the story when they learned of the websites and questions that began popping up about the location.

Being an investigator of all things weird in Oklahoma, you can imagine how these stories sparked my interest. I was determined to go there and check it out and had the rest of the group ready to go, too. I read everything I could find online about it and I began contacting everyone with an email link. Oddly, my emails bounced back to me. Then one day I got an answer. The following is what took place, via email:

"OK, you are the third person I have tried to email about this - all the other ones failed. I have been researching Beaver Sands and it is getting extremely odd that anyone that had a report about it can no longer be contacted. I am the founder of a paranormal investigation team in NW Oklahoma and we were talking about going there and with all these reports of men in black and whatnot, it's becoming even more intriguing. Have you had anything weird happen since you posted the information on the internet?

I would like to know more about this place.

Thanks.

Tammy - Eerie Oklahoma"

I received a reply:

"DO NOT GO THERE! Forget you ever heard about the Beaver Sands portal. Anyone who ever knew anything is now gone... be safe. I am not in the country so do not try to find me. Do me a favor and ask no one about me. You may already be monitored if you are asking questions. This isn't a game... seriously give it up. DT"

Of course I was somewhat rattled by this response, but not enough to be deterred from my investigation. I shared it with the team and it only made us want to go that much more. The next day, I got this email in my inbox:

"It is not a healthy interest to involve yourself. Endeavors of this nature are best left to those who understand the risks. Beaver, Oklahoma has an abundance of predators in its Sand Dunes. It also has an equal abundance of victims buried beneath them. Not a threat... Just advice.

A friend"

This was totally bizarre and even more intriguing. So I replied. What follows is the correspondence between this "friend" and me.

"So what's going on out there and who are you and how do you know? How did you know I was looking into it - you weren't one of the people I inquired of?"

The Reply:

"If anyone were to make inquiry of events in Beaver, Oklahoma I would be the first person to know. I know quite a lot about you... Tammy.

Miss Eerie Oklahoma, eh? Born March of 1973... the places on Broadway... Randolph... Coolidge... Etc., etc. Enid is a nice town. Saw your picture on the website...pretty Girl.

Anyway...

This isn't one of your pleasant little jaunts into the back roads. You get involved here and you will find yourself way over your head. Trust me...take my advice. None of this is meant as a threat. I truly am being your friend. People a lot more visible than you are now invisible.

Davis Humes"

This reply seemed odd to me because I am pretty much an open book, plus, I do a lot of research, so I know how easy it is to find these answers about people. We went further:

"None of those things are hard to find out about me - I am a pretty public person. Your emails do sound like threats to me even if you state they aren't. You say it is friendly advice - why would you be concerned and why all the high drama to try to scare me?"

His reply:

"Well Warnings and drama didn't scare me either. Wish they had. Read the below link and you will understand I am a friend.
http://www.100megsfree4.com/farshores/beaver.htm"

Still not scared enough to drop the subject, I persist:

"I read an account about that. It says you wish someone would seriously investigate it."

Then I received this ever so interesting reply:

"That was years ago... before a lot of events transpired. Look at the list of investigators who have disappeared

Carrol Hempsted -RUFOA and SETIRP (RUFOA and SETIRP are now defunct)

Stirling Dutchford (Phoenix Foundation , Co-chair of SETIRP)

Dr. Mark Thatcher (Shaman's Portal Author, Phoenix Foundation)

Delbert Trammell (in hiding)

All these were real people who tried to help me. All are gone now (disappeared) with the exception of D. Trammell who had his life turned upside down. This doesn't even include the witnesses who have all

disappeared...including my family members. Davis Humes isn't my real name. It is as if none of them ever existed. This will be my last correspondence with you. I tried to warn you. This address will no longer be valid in a few days.
 Davis"

Over the couple of days that this was going on, I had told my mom and my husband about it and they both became very worried. They wanted me to stop looking into the subject of the portal and just move on, but I couldn't. After I received this last email, my husband was adamant that I drop the subject. I told him it was probably some thirty-four-year-old gamer dude living in his mom's basement in Pennsylvania getting a big kick out of trying to scare me over the Internet. He didn't agree. He was sure we'd be met by some scary guy with a big knife out in the sand dunes, or something worse. I just wasn't buying the whole story because things didn't really add up to me. I was doing research on domain names and analyzing the writing styles and spelling and grammar usage of the writers and things just weren't jiving. I even went so far as to call universities to ask about some of these people. The next morning, I received another email:

"It's hard to keep a straight face... before you waste your time with any of this which would be a shame, it is all a hoax. There never was a Beaver Sands portal. I made it up as a psych experiment in '97 about belief apart from evidence. It got out of hand and I abandoned it in '98. But the internet wouldn't let it die. lol
 No one knows I created it, as well as a good portion of the web sites. It's funny the things people believe in. Well, it did help the tourist trade in Beaver... haha. This should tell people volumes about Roswell. Check the history... no one has ever disappeared. Now go find a real story.
 Davis Humes
 PS: I am also Dell Trammell as well as all the others listed in my previous email. Fun's over."

HA! I KNEW IT! I was just glad that I had actually said as much before he came clean. I was so glad I had persisted in finding out about this story and I was feeling pretty excited about debunking a huge urban legend, too. The rest of the emails follow:

"I would have never made a good MIB anyway... really... I let it die years ago and have done nothing since...but the internet conspiratists won't let it go. It's kinda funny. I tried before to tell folks but they wouldn't believe me... Dreams die hard. Anyway... good luck in the future.
 Davis (Not my real name), your anonymous friend.
 P.S. could I interest you in a slightly used sandy space craft? Lol"

My reply:

"LOL. Obviously, we research things like this and this is a great urban legend now. I am thinking about writing an article on it - would you mind? I can keep my sources anonymous. Or would you rather keep it going? I was kinda hoping you'd take it as far as meeting us in the dunes with some mind zapper looking thing, lol."

What he said next was very interesting and valuable - read it closely.

"Nah. I don't especially want to keep it goin'... but it will, despite what you or I say or do. People like to believe in things like this. My experience has taught me something valuable though...beyond the jokes and the legends there is a hope that people hold onto that goes deeper than facts will ever support. I think that is cool. It is evidence of something more in itself. The experience also tells me that many of the other... (not all) but many of the other urban legends are just as fake. As one who has woven the tapestry, I have begun to recognize the threads of tomfoolery when I see them. I think I would make a decent researcher because of this. I would always be looking for the little man behind the curtain.

Please write about it. And if you include any emails in the article include this one especially.

"Folks... never check your minds with your hats at the door. True faith is almost always fact based. Faith based on wishful thinking is nothing but deception waiting to happen. There will always be someone like me lurking in the shadows with a woolen blanket to pull over your eyes."

I cannot reveal my true self at this time because it would play havoc in my life... don't need it now. I won't have to use the mind zapper. ..unless of course you find me....lol

....Now everyone look into the flashy thing and say "cheese".

Davis Humes"

So there you have it - The Shaman's Portal debunked. What an awesome story, though, huh? Shortly after making this discovery, I was telling a friend about it and he was beside himself. He had actually been out in the Beaver Sands, tromping around in the dunes looking for the portal. Since I began researching this story and found out the truth behind it, the legend has indeed grown and maybe it will continue to do so. I have no idea of the true identity of Davis Humes, but I would definitely like to meet up with him in person someplace and discuss this over a cold beer. In a very well-lit, well-populated place, that is.

THE LADY IN BLACK

Submitted by Roxanne Geddes

When I was in junior high I had a weird experience with something I know I will never forget.

I had been in bed in my loft bedroom on North 10th street in Enid, Oklahoma, around the year 1987. I had been asleep for a few hours when I heard someone calling my name. I was half asleep and figured I was just dreaming. Then someone placed a cold hand firmly on my leg and said my name sternly. When I woke, I saw the most beautiful woman I had ever seen sitting on the corner of my bed by my feet. She was dressed in a black, flowing, princess-style dress - similar to what they wore during the time of King Arthur's court. She had long, straight black hair that flowed down her back. Her skin was fair and smooth and her lips and long fingernails were painted deep red. Her eyes were brown and very gentle.

Beautiful as she was, I was terrified and pulled the covers over my head. I was shaking horribly. She said my name again and told me that my mother needed me and I needed to go downstairs to her immediately.

I started crying and pulled the covers away from face. She was gone.

I looked around and when I didn't see any trace of her, I darted from my bed and ran down the stairs screaming for my mother. What I found will be ingrained in my memory forever.

My mother had been rearranging the furniture in the living room and the couch had fallen on top of her. She was pinned under the couch and couldn't move it by herself. She wasn't hurt or anything; she just needed my help to move the couch off of her and she had been hollering for me.

I have never seen the lady again, but she was as real as you and I standing in the same room talking. I can still to this day see her image in my mind as clearly as I did the night she appeared.

The house we were living in had belonged to two elderly "old maid" sisters, Ruth and Hazel, and one of them had died in that house. They were the sweetest two women ever. I can't say it was either of them because I only knew them as older women, but whoever that lady was, she was an angel of some sort. The old house burned down several years ago but before it did, nothing else out of the ordinary ever happened there.

One night, I was telling this story to my friend at a sleepover. We were in her bed and it was very dark and quiet in the house. I had just finished the story when we heard a voice at the door. We both screamed in terror to see a woman in a long black nightgown standing in the doorway. It was her mother coming to tell us to go to sleep!

A STORMY NIGHT IN ADA
Submitted by Regina Walker

This event takes place in Ada, Oklahoma, my hometown. I think I was about ten or eleven years old at the time. I lived with my great-aunt Flora, who raised me from birth. It was during the springtime = "tornado season" as we call it here. My aunt and I lived in a duplex house, which is still located on West 12th Street. Our side of the duplex sat right next to the street. One night when the weather was particularly bad, I was lying on the couch. My aunt and I used to stay up until the bad weather passed and then go to sleep afterwards. When it was "all clear" in our area, she suggested we go ahead and go to bed.

We had to pass through the kitchen to get to the bedrooms. We were in the living room heading toward the kitchen when we heard a car drive up. The windows were open since it was a warm night so we could hear everything outside very clearly.

By the time we got into the kitchen, we heard the car door slam. It sounded like the car was right outside the kitchen window. "Oh, I bet that's Ewell," Aunt Flora said. Ewell was her brother, my grandfather. My grandfather used to come over when the weather was bad and go with us to the storm cellar across the street because his house had no cellar.

After we heard the car door slam shut, we heard my grandfather, Ewell, call, "Flora?"

Aunt Flora answered, "Yeah?"

She then said to me, "Go to the back door, and I'll go to the front; that way, if he goes to the back, you will be there, or if he goes to the front, I will be there."

I dutifully went to the back door, but my grandfather wasn't there. I went to the front, thinking my grandfather must have gone that way but he wasn't there, either.

"I wonder where he went?" said Aunt Flora, puzzled.

We looked out to see his car, but there was no car parked in the drive.

My Aunt became worried. We'd both heard a car drive up, we'd both heard a car door slam; we'd both heard him call Aunt Flora's name.

My aunt decided to call my grandfather's house. My grandmother answered the phone and my aunt asked if my grandfather was there. My grandmother was taken aback by the urgency in my aunt's voice and asked what was going on. Aunt Flora told my grandmother the story of what had happened, and my grandmother said, "Well, Ewell is in bed. Has been for awhile, and he's fast asleep."

THE SMITH HOUSE

By Tammy Wilson

In 1984, one of the gristliest murders in Enid's history occurred. A prominent businessman, whom I'll call Mr. Smith, known to be homosexual, was attacked and brutally murdered in his home.

On the evening of the murder, he had two young male guests with him. They were in the bedroom watching a movie when someone rang the doorbell. Smith went to answer the door. When he opened it, he was rushed by two men, stabbed repeatedly, and killed as he stood in the entryway of his home.

One of the attackers went to attend to the other two men. As one of the guests was trying frantically to escape through the doors that lead to the outside from the bedroom, he was brutally stabbed. The police later discovered three inches of a filet knife broken off in the man's brain, yet the murderer had continued stabbing him even after the blow to the brain had killed him.

During the melee, the third man seemed to have disappeared. The two cold-blooded killers searched the house and could not locate him anywhere. What they didn't know was that in the bedroom, near the back wall, was a very small cabinet that was not easily seen. The man had quietly slipped into it. He stayed there, sweating and terrified, for five or six hours, his heart beating wildly as he listened to the assailants searching for him.

The next morning, when he felt it was safe, the man left his hiding place and called the police. What they found was a shocking and gory scene. The light-colored bedroom carpet oozed red. There was blood everywhere. The police questioned the man who had reported the crime. They found it hard to believe that with all the blood and mess he had gone unscathed. He told them he had hidden in the cabinet to escape the predators. They wanted to see it, so he showed them. They immediately disbelieved his story; the cabinet was both incredibly narrow and not very tall.

The cabinet is still in the house. I have personally seen it. I could not fathom how a grown man, small or not, could have gotten inside it. The police asked him how he could have possibly gotten in there, let alone hide for so long. He placed his foot on the small table near the cabinet and boosted himself into the cramped space once again. Sure enough, investigators were able to later find a footprint in the back of the cabinet, corroborating the man's story.

After thirteen hours at the bloody crime scene, the police had no hard evidence against anyone, though they had an idea of who the attackers were. Some people who had been in the park adjacent to the house were able to give physical descriptions of the attackers and the car in which they arrived. It was not lost on the police that the attackers were seen wearing gloves yet parked a yellow Camaro right in front of the house. They had obviously intended to leave no witnesses. Without actual evidence, though, it would be difficult to close the case.

The investigators decided the best way to get to the killers would be to find a woman with whom they were close. The best way to get to a man, after all, is through a woman. They located someone they knew to be friendly with one of the suspects and they approached her. She agreed to help them and began calling, visiting, and talking at length with the suspect, all the while with the police listening. Over the weeks she spoke with him, he confessed to her that he'd killed a man in California. He said he had been hitchhiking and a man picked him up. The driver made a sexual advance toward him, so he said he beat him in the head with a wrench until he was dead and left his body in the trees. He claimed to have killed another man in Georgia, leaving the body to rot in a swamp. But he never spoke of the Enid murders.

The woman eventually decided to leave the state, but when she did, she happened to take the investigator's tape recorder with her. They had no way to reach her or get her back, so the investigator approached her sister and told her that if the woman did not return to Oklahoma, he would have to file embezzlement charges against her for taking his tape recorder. Not wanting trouble with the police, the informant returned to Oklahoma. They reminded her that she'd agreed to help them and they expected her to do just that. She said, "Okay, let's do this," and they once again set out to get a confession out of the suspect.

Some days later, the woman contacted the police to let them know the suspect wanted to take her out to the Gloss Mountains, a remote range of mesas in northwestern Oklahoma. They devised a plan to follow and listen, worried that her safety might be in jeopardy. She would be out in the middle of nowhere, with not many nearby places for the police to conceal themselves and get to her in time if anything untoward were to happen. During the trek to the Gloss Mountains, the suspect spilled his guts about the Enid murders and the police were able to get the entire thing on tape, thanks to the informant. They arrested him based on this confession and he was later sentenced to life in prison, where he remains.

The man never testified in Oklahoma about the second man involved in the killings, who had moved on to Texas. He met a woman who had an ex-boyfriend who owned a jewelry store and she thought they could rob it. They went to his house to confront him and demand loot. The killer had fashioned a ten-pound Samurai sword and when the storeowner turned on him, he split him from the shoulder to the navel and ran the sword through his brain as he fell to the ground.

His partner from the Enid mess later testified as to his involvement in the Oklahoma murders when the second man went to trial in Texas for the slaying of the jewelry store owner. The police were able to obtain the transcripts of that trial and wanted to use them to bring action against the second man in Oklahoma, but the victim's family was not interested in opening up old wounds or having to deal with such a high profile case anymore. It was over for them and that's how they wanted it to stay. Even though the second man was never brought to trial in Oklahoma, he was eventually executed in Texas.

Something I have always found particularly odd about this story is that there is only one person left who can tell us what happened that night and he is in prison. His defense attorney passed away, the man who hid in the cabinet dead also, and the second man involved in the killings has been executed.

After the murders, the family of the victim took over the house and eventually lived there for several years until another family bought it. A few years ago, I was contacted by a teenage boy who told me, "I think my house is haunted." We began to talk about the things that were happening at his house and why he would think it was haunted. His mother worked out of town and was gone a lot and his father no longer lived in the house, so the boy was there on his own quite often. His house was the place where all his friends crashed and when they eventually started a band, they would practice there as well. There was never a shortage of teenage boys around the place. Several of them told me stories of glimpsing someone in the kitchen and finding no one there when they went to investigate. They also said they had heard unexplained noises and experienced other odd things while in the house.

As they continued to fill me in on the happenings at the house, they told me what disturbed them most was they would often be awakened by an unseen someone playing with their hair or touching their faces.

When I asked where this house was located so I could do some historical research, the boy who had first told me about the haunting said, "Oh, you probably know the house; it's the Smith house." Aha! Things were starting to make sense...

The preceding story is true and the facts are accurate. I was able to interview the police investigator who worked this case. I knew the occupant of the house and was able to tour it with the investigator. The story of the killings has been told in my hometown since it happened, when I was a child. It was fascinating for me to be able to learn more about it from the people who knew the most. I have, however, changed the name of the first victim and not mentioned the names of either the second victim or the murderers. People in Enid will know the story anyway, but I wanted to respect the families of the victims and not bring attention to the criminal or danger upon myself by putting his name in a book.

TRICK OR TREAT?

By Penn King

We bought our home on Halloween, 2005. That night we were met with a gas leak, plumbing leaks and a gizmo that kept beeping to let the mice know it somehow knew of their presence, and would somehow do something about it. One doorjamb defied gravity, and the keys we were handed at closing matched none of the locks in the doors. It was an auspicious beginning for a journey that led to meeting at least one comforting, if not clearly seen, new friend. Trick or treat!

My mother and I live in the childhood home of the late Marvella Bayh (wife of Senator Birch Bayh and mother of Senator Evan Bayh of Indiana). In her book, Marvella, a Personal Journey, she described the house as a place where she had many happy years with her mother and father. We knew nothing about any of this when we bought the house, only that it suited our needs. While on the whole we felt welcomed, there was one room that no one, not even the dogs or cats wanted anything to do with. The dining room seemed to have a foreboding "just pass on by" feeling to it, and everyone seemed relieved to do that. About the only residents in the room were occasional packages placed on the table, and the echoes of our quick footsteps going to or from the kitchen.

Months later my ex-husband called and asked what our street address was. I told him and he said that we were living in a house mentioned in a few books about Oklahoma. I went online and sure enough, our home was mentioned as the address of the late Delbert Murphy Hern, Marvella's father. I learned that he had been involved in at least two paranormal study groups, had raised his family in relative contentment in the home, lost his first wife, and had married another woman some years his junior. The second marriage wasn't a happy one. One March night in 1970, the sixty-year-old Hern shot his second wife to death as she sat at the dining room table. Moments later, in the area under the archway between the living and dining rooms, he took his own life.

That explained a great deal about the cold, unhappy feeling of the dining room. What we couldn't figure out was why the rest of the house felt so absolutely charming. Having grown up in a world of spirits and shadows, the tapping on the kitchen table and the woman's voice speaking incessantly for long moments at a time (sounding like a radio that was tuned just a bit too low to make out what she was talking about) were seen as more a reason for comfort than concern. Sometimes small items would disappear within seconds of putting them down. These events indicated a more caring, sometimes teasing spirit than a man who had so tragically ended two lives.

Having carefully cleaned the house of negativity, the dining room now feels like one in your average house - just a dining room. We're all pleased though, that the woman keeps letting us know she's there. Could it be Marvella? Recently, she spoke to my mother, in a voice as clear as her own, assuring her that she was welcomed and safe in the house. My mum checked all possible sources of the voice, as did her dog who, hearing the words, led the way in trying to find the speaker. Sometimes, you just have to smile and say, "Thank you," and let it go at that.

When I read Marvella's book, I understood her love of the place. Her spirit and her loving memories of life here shone in each page. Who knows? Perhaps our ghost is her mother, or grandmother, both of whom also lived here. Perhaps it's a previous occupant, from even earlier days. We may never be curious enough to investigate who she is and right now it's fine just having her here. Even the pets, watching whoever she is cross the room occasionally, don't seem to mind. Only one of the cats seems to show any concern and as long as she can hurl herself at someone and curl up for safety (peeking out to continue watching), she's content. As are the rest of us, the seen and unseen dwellers of a most charming home.

OKLAHOMA'S OWN DEAD MAN'S CURVE

Submitted by my friend and brother-in-law, someone I know to be honest and trustworthy and who claims not to believe in "stuff like this" - Tammy Wilson

First off, let me preface this by saying just how much of a disbeliever I am about ghost stories and the supernatural. Everyone that knows me knows I am a total naysayer about stuff like that. Having said that...

On Sunday, April 17, 2004, I embarked on a motorcycle ride with several friends to a motorcycle rally. Nothing was out of the ordinary that day other than a rather severe version of the Oklahoma wind forcing us to be at the top of our riding game in order to stay pointed straight down the road. We arrived at the rally, then decided to leave and take a short ride around Waynoka to find some lunch. A few minutes into the trip, disaster struck. My recall of the event is pretty brief, but it includes riding up a gradual hill and curve and my next memory is roughly thirty minutes later being loaded into an ambulance and one of my friends asking for my wife's phone number. Later details from my riding buddy, who was directly behind me, include finding out that everything looked normal to him. I topped the hill and went out of sight, he followed a few seconds later. Upon seeing me again, I was in a severe case of headshake with my handlebars going from full lock one direction and then the other. It eventually ended with me going off the road, flipping several times, and ending up about fifty feet from my motorcycle, just short of plunging through a barbwire fence.

No cause was ever found for the wreck. I was not cited by the highway patrol. My speed was in no way excessive, the wind was not overly gusty at the time it occurred; there seemed to be no reason for the wreck. I have no problem admitting if I screwed up and caused my own demise, but nothing seemed to point in that direction.

I was talking to a friend and co-worker about this event some time later. He grew up on a farm a few miles from where I went down. I explained to him that after I had the wreck I had talked with several people who had either had wrecks or knew someone who had one in that same spot. After a few minutes of discussion, we got out the map and I showed my friend where I had the accident. According to him, that small stretch of road near there has always had a lot of bad and even fatal wrecks. Apparently I went down right in front of an area the locals used to refer to as "Nigger Hill" - it was the location of a hanging tree.

Kind of eerie.

Armed with that new little tidbit of knowledge, I was telling the story to another friend of mine and his father one night. As it turns out, his dad was involved in a head-on collision with another car in that same spot in the late 1960s. He was the only one out of four passengers in the car who survived the accident.

To backtrack to my accident, being a bit of a motor head and having no explanation as to why I crashed that morning, I began looking into mechanical failures on the motorcycle. Something had to have gone wrong that day for me to go from enjoying a leisurely ride with friends to taking soil samples with my face and no recollection of what occurred in between. Frame trueness was checked, motor to transmission to rear wheel alignment was checked, swing arm bearings and steering head bearings were replaced although nothing seemed awry with the old ones. In short I was finding nothing wrong with the bike that pointed towards a mechanical failure.

To further add to the story, I talked to yet another friend who lives in Waynoka after finding out about that hill. I asked him if he had ever heard of that place and his answer was, "Of course." I told him that was where I had my wreck and he immediately just said, "Well, now you know what happened to you. I wouldn't worry at all about something being wrong with your bike, I live there and I don't go down that road."

Very strange.

The locals all seem fairly convinced it is a cursed road that consumes its share of motorcycle riders and automobile drivers. Also, I dragged out my photos of the wreck and took them to my friend from Waynoka to see. In the shot where they took a picture of the skid marks, there is a huge tree in the background. He claims that is the tree. As soon as he flipped to that picture he said, "Yep, there it is," and pointed to this lone tree in the background of the photo.

Kind of spooky... If you believe in that kind of stuff!

ELKS LODGE NO. 743

Rock Island Ave.
El Reno, Oklahoma
By Tonya Hacker

The Lodge of the Benevolent and Protective Order of the Elks, overlooking historic Route 66, attracts attention as one drives into El Reno. The white stucco building remains unseasoned in appearance, despite nearly a century of exposure to the Oklahoma weather. It is a fine example of the city's numerous historical structures. However, this rather unassuming lodge harbors a unique history as well as a collection of playful ghosts.

Originally constructed as the Oklahoma Territorial Building at the Louisiana Purchase Exposition of 1904, informally known as the St. Louis World Fair, the structure was slated for demolition following the closing of the fair. It attracted the attention of El Reno resident and Elks Lodge member, Otto Shuttee, who moved to save the attraction from its fate. Shuttee contracted for the two-story structure to be cut into sections, loaded onto flatbed railcars, and shipped to El Reno via the Rock Island Railroad. Transportation and reassembling the building took a year to complete, but on November 20, 1905, it entered its new life as the official home of Elks Lodge No. 743.

Lodge members exhibit an ardent devotion to the traditions of the fraternal society. The Elks Lodge, while harboring strong ties to community and nation, remains a social organization at its core. To honor the heart of the order, Elks participate in an 11:00 p.m. ritual known as the Eleven O'clock Toast. It is a time members take to recognize the bond that ties fellow Elks, living and dead. In the words of the toast, it is the "golden hour of reflection." An early version of the Elks' toast, penned in 1896 by Dr. C.H. Harvey, contains the following lines: "...and Jack, who died a year ago when life was in its summer; I see him in the shadows now, a new and welcome comer. Dear boys! I know not where you are, nor do I care to ponder, on your home in that far land across the fairy yonder; but yet I know where'er you are, you'd hurry out of heaven, to drink this toast with those you love when the clock points to eleven."

The toast always seems to cause a supernatural stir, and little wonder considering the bond between Elks and the daily vigils held in memory of absent members. No wonder so many Elks opt to return to their lodge in spirit; who, involved in such camaraderie, would want to leave?

There is no need to be frightened as one explores the lodge; the

The Elks Lodge in El Reno, Oklahoma

reported incidents demonstrate the ghosts are friendly and often of a playful nature. While encountering departed members is unnerving, most Elks later recall their experiences with amusement and the spirits have become a frequent topic of conversation. Functions at the lodge trigger paranormal activity and most of the reported encounters occur following events such as parties and meetings. One story told to the investigators demonstrates how well established the spirits are in the lodge.

Closing up one evening following a steak dinner party, two newer members of the Elks heard big band music descending from the ballroom. The woman and a companion headed upstairs to see why the music played after closing time. The music ceased as they approached the stairs and upon reaching the top, the two found only darkness and a vacant ballroom. Spooked and uneasy about their experience, they hurriedly closed up the lodge and left. Days later, after the tension of what happened had receded, the two confronted their fellow members about the ghostly party in the ballroom wherein they learned that it was not an isolated event. The older Elks nonchalantly informed the two young Elks that it happens regularly to those who spend a considerable amount of time there, but only when it is least expected. Such paranormal gatherings are just one of the strange yet wonderful reminders of the parties that have occurred over the past century at the Elks Lodge.

The ghosts are not shy towards non-Elks, despite their attraction to fellow members, as the Lodge's guests have experienced. The El Reno Elks offered Oklahoma-based ghost hunting team GHOULI (Ghost Haunts of Oklahoma and Urban Legends Investigations) the privilege of investigating their lodge and its paranormal claims. The Elks extended complete access to the team, who spent hours trying to capture evidence of the rumored spirits, but once again, the spirits so familiar with the building, managed to catch the team off guard.

The ghostly tales usually consist of humorous episodes centered in the bar area. Barkeeps and patrons state it is common for the pesky spirits to make their presence known in numerous ways. Startled guests have witnessed the jukebox come to life, playing familiar tunes of yesterday, despite being unplugged from the outlet. Cigarettes have been flicked or put out, while others have had their drinks spilled or slid down the bar by an unknown source. The dim mirrors behind the bar are purported to be a means to glimpse into the lodge's past, and as one Elk informed the author, "If you sit long enough, you will see people walking behind you that haven't lived in years." This, of course, could be caused from the consumption of spirits of another sort, but then again, it could possibly be the ghosts of departed Elks bellying up for last call.

The bar is not the building's only active area. Sporadic coughs descending from nowhere and random laughter echoing down empty halls have kept the Elks aware of their lodge's haunted status and intrigue member and guest alike.

GHOULI spent many hours investigating the historical building in August 2006. The team divided the investigation into different parts in order to try and validate as many of the claims as possible and several bizarre occurrences surprised the skeptical members. During the investigation, two team members heard footstep ascending the main staircase, despite no one being on the third floor. The team remained stationary in their designated locations in an attempt to isolate the noise, but the footsteps continued, prompting one investigator to comment, "Nobody was walking around the lodge, well, nobody that was alive."

At one point in the evening, in the top-floor private bar area, one investigator tested the common report of cigarettes being flicked and beers being spilt. She lit a cigarette and placed it in an ashtray and placed a beer on the bar prior to leaving the room. When she returned a short time later, the beer remained untouched, but the unattended cigarette had been moved and its ashes apparently flicked.

Later in the investigation, one of the more skeptical team members ventured off to explore the main floor where billiards and poker tables provide entertainment for the Elks. The rooms are away from the main hall and are generally kept private, so the investigator asked if he should close the door when he exited. A female Elk member in the poker room responded that it didn't matter, but he closed the door anyway. Later on, when investigators analyzed the tape in the recorder he carried, a third voice appeared in the conversation that was had not been heard either by the Elk or the investigator. Following the question about the door, a male voice interjects and states in a firm, yet mild tone, "Yes." After reviewing the tape, the investigator was glad that he actually did shut the door, lest he should offend some unseen Elk.

The lower floor has a regularly reported paranormal occurrence in the most surprising of places: the women's restroom. A reoccurring story is that when women are in the stalls, they hear a woman in heels enter the restroom. Some have seen stall doors open, others have heard the toilets flushed by some unseen force. Some have even called out to the unknown person and innocently asked for tissue, only to be shocked when they discover no one is in the restroom with them. One of the female investigators tested the story late in the evening, but, after waiting patiently for some time, she actually felt the need to utilize the facilities. As she sat in the stall, she heard what she thought to be another team member enter the room to check on her. After wondering for a few moments why the other woman didn't answer, it dawned on her that she was, in fact, alone and had become the latest in experiencing the phenomenon. Shaken, she left the restroom and abandoned her experiment for the evening.

"Things happen when you least expect it," are words to heed when dealing with the ghosts of the Elks Lodge in El Reno.

True to the Elks' claims, the ghosts of the lodge departed as the building was shut down for the evening. Spirits of the Elks seem to enjoy themselves more when there are plenty of people around for them to socialize with. The honoring of tradition seems to play a role in maintaining the level of paranormal activity, as demonstrated by the Eleven O'clock Toast. Phantoms of yesterday still enjoy the custom, and probably appreciate the respect given to their memory. Everyone at the lodge agrees that without the active camaraderie of the Elks that honors the past, the ghosts would not make themselves such a distinct presence in the old building.

The spirits of the Elks Lodge do not wander aimlessly, but rather make a conscious choice to make their presence known when they feel it is necessary. The faces of former Elks line the walls in portraits, but which departed member is actually going to show up is open for questioning. One Elk states, "Sometimes, certain members show up while others don't," as if the rotating ghosts of the lodge visit to check in on their fellow members and possibly play a few pranks on them. In turn, the members are reminded of the tradition, brotherhood and Elk credence that make the halls of Elks Lodge No. 743 such a special place for so many, both present and departed.

GRANNY'S HOUSE
By Tammy Wilson

The big Queen Ann-style house on West Broadway was built in 1910 and changed hands a few times before the Johnson Family acquired it in 1956. At that time, Dr. and Mrs. Howard Johnson and their daughter, Dr. Jeanne Johnson, lived there. They had another daughter, Jayne, Jeanne's identical twin, who was married and had a family and did not live in the house. However, she did spend much time there, as did her family.

Howard Johnson was the first of the family to pass away and then Jeanne, followed by Mrs. Johnson, whom the family called Granny. Among family members, the house is known as "Granny's House." Jayne was the only survivor of Dr. Johnson's immediate family for many years.

Jayne was my step-grandmother and she had inherited the house. In the late fall of 1996, my husband and I moved in. There were still some of the original antique furnishings, which we used, and there was a big portrait of Dr. Howard Johnson hanging on the dining room wall. We felt it only proper and respectful to leave it there, as it had been his house, after all. We were expecting a new baby in the spring and we were excited to begin our family in this grand old home. When we first moved in, we heard doors banging and noises coming from upstairs quite frequently. Then after a while it stopped. We assumed it was Aunt Jeanne's ghost and once she realized we were family, she stopped trying to scare us.

The baby arrived and her room was upstairs directly across from ours. Sometimes at night, footsteps would be heard over the baby monitor. I would frantically run to check on the baby only to find everything as it should be.

As it usually is when a newborn comes home, the mother doesn't get a lot of sleep. One morning I woke up and realized that I had slept through the entire night. At first, I was excited to think that my baby was finally starting to sleep through the night and then I became worried. I quickly went to check on things and the baby was fine and sleeping soundly. I returned to my room and inspected the baby monitor. It was turned off. Neither my husband nor I ever turned off the baby monitor. We often wondered if perhaps Aunt Jeanne was watching over us and knew that as a new mom I was tired and needed rest so she turned the monitor off to let me sleep.

Jayne, Jeanne's twin, had moved in down the street with my parents and our family visited them frequently. My daughter came to know her as Nana Jayne. When our second daughter came along, we moved our oldest child from the nursery into the room next to ours -- Jeanne's old room. One summer day when the baby was about 18 months old, she was sitting on the bed in her room. Keep in mind that Jeanne had passed away long before and no one in our house then had ever met her. The child looked up at the doorway as if someone had just walked into the room and said, "Hi. Hi, Nana Jayne."

There was no one there. The hair on my neck stood up and my skin crawled because I knew who she had seen - Jeanne and Jayne were identical twins and if the child had seen Jeanne, she would assume it was Jayne, not knowing any different.

Another time the same child, a couple of years later, woke up in the night claiming that someone had sat on her bed and woke her up and she didn't want to sleep in there anymore. She had several bad dreams and would never talk about them, except once, when she claimed there was a scary man at the bottom of the stairs.

One night, I was in bed asleep and was awakened to the sound of sobbing. I got up and checked on the kids and found them all sleeping soundly. I walked through the entire house. I couldn't find where the crying was coming from. There were drive-through restaurants on either side of the house and I thought perhaps voices from the intercoms were carrying. I went out the front door - nothing. I went out the back door - nothing. I woke my husband and made him go look with me. He could not hear it and thought I was crazy. After I looked everywhere, I finally gave up and went back to bed, but I could still hear those sobs. It bothered me for about an hour before I finally went back to sleep. When I woke up again a couple of hours later the crying had stopped.

Later when I questioned the family about whether they'd ever experienced the sobs, I learned that Jeanne had had a fiancé who had been killed in a car accident and she had spent a significant amount of time crying over his loss.

When we had been living there about six years, the family decided they had to sell the house and we had to move out. We moved across town and my daughter's bad dreams stopped. For a period of about a year the house was unoccupied, and eventually we offered to buy it. We decided that while the house was empty, we would remodel and have some work done before moving back in.

Right before we were going to move back in, my mother asked me about having a séance there. I said absolutely not, as I didn't want to stir anything up. I asked her what prompted her to want to have the séance,

She told me that while my uncle was in the house doing some repair work, he confided to her that he heard noises and voices upstairs. When he went upstairs to confront whoever was in the house, he said he found no one there. One evening my mother had gone there to get something out of the house. She heard banging upstairs and yelled, "It's just me. I'll be gone in a minute," at which time the banging stopped.

Another time, a friend of the family took her son and her boyfriend to tour the house with her. It was the middle of summer in Oklahoma, which translates to being deadly still and hot in the house. When they approached the landing on the second floor, the prisms on the ceiling light fixture began shaking violently. Now, I had lived in this house for years and never witnessed anything like that, even when the adjacent attic fan was on. There was no wind at all this day. The two grown men turned and ran out of the house. The woman spoke out loud and told the house she was a friend, and it stopped. She reported that she felt like whatever caused the prisms to tremble was not necessarily friendly.

One night, I had to go into the house and get something. I got an uneasy feeling as I went up the stairs. I had lived in this house for a long time and I loved it, so I was not normally scared there. But this night was different. I was spooked for some reason. I went into the room to get what I had come for when I was consumed with what can only be described as a "Get the hell outta here" feeling. I literally ran out of the house.

So, with these rather unnerving things taking place since the house had become empty, I was a little apprehensive about moving my children back into it. I contacted a paranormal investigation team to come check it out. They did and what they found was very interesting to say the least. During the time the house was unoccupied, Jayne passed away, so now all of the original Johnson family was gone. When the investigative team was there, they recorded a woman's voice saying, "Hello" in the same exact manner as Jayne always said it. It was so much like her voice that it brought several family members to tears when they heard it.

Another interesting thing about that recording is that there was a heartbeat that preceded the voice. They tried to recreate recording a heartbeat and were not successful. The recording was sent to a cardiologist to analyze. The doctor told them it was the heartbeat of someone with congestive heart failure, which Jayne had.

The team was able to validate that the house was possibly haunted but did not feel there was anything particularly menacing there. However, when I returned to my house across town after the investigation that night, I had something very odd happen.

No one was home when I got there. I went in the front door and directly to the back door to let the dog out. I waited for him and he followed me back into the living room, where I lay down on the couch. Our dog, Slurpie, was a big boxer. He stood in front of me and looked over me at something behind me; the hair on his back bristled up and he began to bark angrily. I tried to get his attention but he ignored me. I called his name a few times, but he was focused on something behind me. I finally grabbed his collar on both sides, trying to get him to look at me, but he wouldn't. He was clearly upset about something and frankly I was too frightened to look behind me to see what it was. After a minute, Slurpie stopped barking and turned away. All I know is that from that day forward, whatever was unfriendly at the big Broadway house was gone. I think it followed me home, freaked my dog out, and went on its way.

We moved back in to the house on Broadway a few months later and it seemed to us that the negative feelings were indeed gone.

Things went well and there were no odd occurrences. We chalked it up to the house being happy we were back home. Then one night, I was in my room putting away laundry when my oldest daughter, the one who had had all the prior experiences, yelled, "What?"

"What, what?" I replied.

She came walking into my room and said, "You called me. What did you want?"

I had not called her. She said she clearly heard me call her name.

Another night, my husband had gone in to read her a bedtime story. I went to bed and fell asleep. Later that night, my husband frantically woke me up. He was obviously flustered and I asked him what the matter was. He said he had fallen asleep in her room and was awakened by my voice whispering to him, "Marty, get up and come to bed." He said he heard it a couple of times, but when he got up, I was not there and he found me sound asleep in our bed. He swore it was my voice.

My grandmother came to my house every morning to care for my children while I worked. I was in the upstairs bathroom one morning doing my hair when I heard her call my name from the bottom of the stairs. I yelled back, "What?" She didn't answer and I figured it wasn't that important. I finished getting ready and went downstairs. She was coming out of the kitchen and I asked her what she had hollered at me about. She looked at me and said, "I just walked in the back door, I didn't holler at you."

I became a little frightened that three different people in my house had heard their names called by a familiar voice that did not belong to any of us. Other than that, there were no other unusual experiences. We ended up only living there a year and a half before we moved into my husband's family home. My cousin took over the old Johnson family house. When they were getting ready to move in, she asked me not to tell her husband about any of the odd things we had experienced because she didn't think he would stay there if he knew about them. But if things are still happening, it's more than likely just her departed relatives keeping things interesting.

I did tell her it might be a good idea to leave the portrait of Dr. Johnson on the dining room wall, just in case.

OKLAHOMA'S PHANTOM HITCHHIKERS
By Tonya Hacker

I have always had a fear of traveling alone late at night. One reason for my fear is due to the ghostly roadside specter stories that I have heard ever since childhood. You know the stories: out on the road you pick up a hitchhiker later to realize he or she was, in fact, a ghost. Even more frightening are the tales of apparitions suddenly jumping out in front of automobiles, startling the drivers and causing them to veer off the road and crash. I have always suspected that these stories and others like them were cautionary tales, invented by parents of teenagers trying to ensure their fledging drivers were safe and alert behind the wheel. Or better yet, to keep kids in the house after dark. No matter what the origins of these tales, they are an interesting part of history in the state of Oklahoma.

During my years of investigating I have received countless emails from people who claimed to have encountered one of these so-called phantom hitchhikers. I started to pay more attention to them after I interviewed a woman who told me about her experience with a roadside specter. In her late forties, this woman had a respected career and did not strike me as someone who would exaggerate or make up stories. It was obvious she felt uncomfortable telling me what had happened to her. She kept repeating, "You are not going to believe me." As an investigator, I have learned that when people are hesitant about sharing their stories, or better yet, if they are trying to convince themselves of a reasonable explanation for their experience, it is a sure-fire sign that they are probably speaking about a true and authentic paranormal event.

The woman told me that her ghastly evening began with a phone call from her daughter, a new mother who was feeling overwhelmed. Being a good grandma, she jumped in her truck and headed to help out with the new baby. She was wide-awake and slightly wound up from the despair in her daughter's voice. It was a cold evening and it was slightly sleeting on top of harsh frozen winds. She had to travel about twenty miles into town, a part of rural life to which she had grown accustomed over the years. As she headed down the road the sleet started to get heavier; the windshield wipers were only spreading the ice around instead of keeping her view clear. She eventually slowed down so her defroster could keep up with the ice that seemed to be falling harder with every mile. She eventually slowed down to about twenty mph when she noticed a figure walking on the side of the road. It was a young woman and she seemed to be in trouble, wearing nothing but an oversized man's dress shirt, with bare feet and soaking wet hair. Concerned, she pulled to the side of the road, rolled the passenger-side window down, and asked the girl if she would like a ride into town. The girl nodded and stood waiting for her to open the door.

The young woman was cold, her lips blue and trembling. The woman driving the truck hoisted herself up in her seat and pulled the Indian blanket that acted as a seat cover from underneath her. As the girl climbed in, she handed her the blanket and slowly started to drive. She attempted several times to make small talk, asking her passenger where she was headed or if she was in trouble, but the girl appeared not to want to talk. She glanced down at the girl's bare feet and noticed that they were bleeding and burrs were wedged into the skin. The woman continued to ask her where she wanted to be dropped off once they made it to town. She had a friend in the police department to whom she could take her, being uncertain if the young woman had been in a domestic fight or some kind of car accident. She decided her passenger was not ready to talk but as she approached mile marker forty-seven on the main road about three miles from town, the girl spoke. In a soft breathy voice, jittery from the cold, she said that she was close to home. The woman was happy to hear the girl speak and she was excited to find out where she was to take her. The suspense grew as they passed yet another mile marker; then the young woman spoke again, very softly and hesitantly, "You could turn left on forty-nine. My dad is waiting for me there."

Approaching the mile marker, the woman looked for a house or some place to drop her off. She slowed down and turned on her bright headlights, noticing the ice collecting on her windshield was starting to alter her vision. Suddenly, the girl exclaimed, "Right here, stop here!" Confused, the woman stopped. There were no lights anywhere and no houses in sight. The girl quickly climbed out of the truck and said, "Thank you for the blanket, and please be careful; this road is very dangerous." Then she slammed the door and ran right in front of the truck. The woman watched as she leaped about three feet in front of the headlights and just vanished.

The woman put her truck in park, frightened of what she had just seen. She was overwhelmed with worry as the barefoot girl was nowhere to be found. She rolled down her driver's side window and peered into the trees towards the left side of the road. She then looked down and noticed there was something wedged in the brush. She got out of the truck and crossed the road to get a closer look. She moved a stick or two and noticed a roadside memorial in the shape of a cross. There was no writing on the cross, but she knew that it probably marked the scene of a tragic car accident. The cross was covered with overgrown weeds and some of the plastic flowers had fallen off. She reattached the flowers and pondered what had just happened. She stood there, lingering in amazement for what seemed to be an eternity. Then, coming to her senses, she quickly jumped into her truck and finally made it into town.

She didn't mention what had just happened to her when she arrived at her daughter's house; her daughter was already stressed out with the new baby. She ended up staying the night, both to help out and because she was a little fearful about driving back home on that road. The next morning before heading back home she stopped at the convenience store to fill up on gas and to grab a cup of coffee. Being Sunday morning, traffic was light and it seemed that everyone was in church. As she was filling up her tank an older man was topping off his gas containers. He said good morning to her and she returned the greeting. As she started to get into her truck the man asked her if she was heading down Route 77. She told him yes, she lived out that way and was going home after visiting her daughter in town. Gazing at her with sorrowful eye, the old man said, "I have a daughter. She is no longer with us, but be careful; that road is dangerous." The woman was in disbelief, as the events of the previous evening flashed before her eyes. She thanked him for the warning and hesitantly told him that his daughter was fine now.

Heading down the road back home, she broke down in tears as she passed the mile marker where she had last seen the girl. She told me she didn't want to tell the man that she had actually met his daughter because she felt it wasn't her place to do so. Later on, she said, she found the newspaper article that told the story about a young girl's untimely death. As she examined the photo in the obituary she recognized the girl to whom she had given the ride. She was saddened by the unfortunate event but she also felt a sense of pride being able to relay such an important message to a grieving father who never got to say good-bye to his little girl.

Among the many stories and urban legends that have been told to me as a paranormal researcher, that was probably one of the most heart wrenching of them all. Those are the kinds of stories that separate the miraculous moments in life from the sometimes more lurid ghostly tales that we are quick to scout out as ghost hunters. The woman told me that she never saw the girl on the road again. She feels in her heart the young woman can now cross over, after succeeding in getting a message to her father.

I have heard my fair share of wacky stories over the years, from naked hitchhikers to ghastly goblins slicing apart tires with their wickedly sharp claws. Some of the more amazing stories are still told by many. I have adopted a lot of these tales to share with my children as we are driving late at night. So far, they enjoy them, and always ask for more. I recently realized the importance of these stories as I recalled sharing similar spooky tales on car trips with my father when I was a child. The obvious reason for the stories is to engage the children's attention for a short while, just to stop the pleas of "are we there yet?" and squelch the backseat bickering that can drive a parent to a level of insanity that has yet to be categorized by psychiatrists. Portable DVD players and video games have replaced these old sources of on-the-road entertainment. To me, it is rather sad how a potential memory for a child can be ripped away by an electronic gadget. The beauty of throwing a little scare into your child has been forgotten for the sake of convenience. When was the last time you told spooky tales and allowed your children to use their imaginations while riding in the car? A lot of the phantom hitchhiker legends (I must confess the mass majority of them) are simply made up, but with a little childlike belief, a creative imagination, and a short drive home on a murky road, these tales come alive and will live on in the hearts of children and adults forever.

Someone asked me about a story they had read about the Mother Road - Route 66 --between El Reno and Weatherford. The tale was new to me so I made a quick search and found a short article about the mother road tale. The story is based on what I have compared to the famous Spy vs. Spy characters in Mad magazine. Many people traveling this stretch of road have noticed a man wearing a brown trench coat with a hat pulled down over his eyes. Of course the man is spotted more frequently on rainy or foggy nights, just to add to the trepidation. Some people have reported pulling over to pick up what they assumed to be an older gentleman with car trouble. Once the man is in the car for a short time, he makes a mad leap for freedom while the car is at top speed. He rarely speaks to these eyewitnesses but he makes an unforgettable impression on them after diving headfirst out of their car like a super hero.

Now, it is quite possible that at some point in history a man matching the leaping stranger's description could have perished on this road. As we all know, car accidents happen all the time, so historically speaking it could be possible that such a character did in fact exist. What astounds me the most is the story itself. Could a tale like this one have been made up by a stressed-out parent just trying to make it home without being driven around the bend by the sound of her children bickering in the backseat? Anything is possible. If you are traveling down the Mother Road between El Reno and Weatherford just be aware of the man in the trench coat. If you stop and pick him up, you may want to refrain from going above ten miles per hour, just to see if you can milk him for some information about who he is before he takes a dive out of your passenger door.

A lot of legends are told in the area west of Oklahoma City. The outskirts of El Reno seem to be a hotspot for roadside phantoms and creepy creatures. Perhaps you made a wrong turn while visiting the local casino or perhaps something else told you to make that wrong turn?

While traveling the outskirts of the historic town many people have reported seeing shadows lurk along the roadside. With the land originally belonging to the Cheyenne-Arapaho tribe, they are very open about their mystical superstitions. Some people have reported seeing what appear to be shadow people walking across and even beside the road. Other drivers report seeing people, many people, appearing to be dressed in black and just wandering around as if they were lost or searching for something. The locals are strong believers in shadow people; not the hokey red-eyed monsters created by fiction writers, but shadows of people from the past, the keepers and original habitants of the land. There is a lot of controversy behind the shadow people phenomenon but I won't get into that because this chapter is about roadside ghosts. Driving along the back roads of El Reno or the Concho Reservation, do not be surprised if you catch a glimpse of shadows from the past moving over the flat lands. They are nothing more than shadows that reflect what life used to be many years ago.

In the same area, local lore and legends are still going strong. Bigfoot has been spotted on the outskirts of this western town for decades. Locals call him The Creature. Tales of oversized elusive monkeys also circulate in the area and most of the locals are devoted believers and trackers of the Giant Man Monkey. There are many eyewitness accounts, including my own originating from the back roads of western Oklahoma.

Many years ago, when I was new to the whole concept of ghost hunting, my team and I were invited to investigate a house far west of El Reno. We headed out shortly after dusk to find the haunted residence, which was located (appropriately enough) in the town of Hitchcock. I will admit that I am an apprehensive but adventurous driver. What that means is that while I am focused on finding our destination, I am also a fan of staying off the main roads during my travels. I like to take my time and enjoy the scenery and small town charm that are bypassed by the main freeway.

We were having a great time while traveling the long route, seeing the sights and absorbing the suspense of the evening's ghost hunt. We were about twenty miles west of El Reno when out of the corner of my eye I saw a large black figure lurking in a moonlit pasture about one hundred yards away. I yelled out in surprise and asked if anyone had seen what I just saw. Of course they all told me to stop and go back. One of my team members is an avid Bigfoot researcher and she insisted that I had seen him. I have never been a big believer in the so-called Sasquatch legend in Oklahoma until that night. Unfortunately fear overcame me and I continued to drive. If in fact there is such a thing as Bigfoot, I was not prepared to meet him face to face. My imagination started to run wild and people who know me personally realize that I have a deep fear of "The Creature." As my teammates insisted I turn back, I continued to think about what I had seen in the pasture. It was large and powerful in appearance, even from afar. I made the choice then and there that I didn't want to be the person who actually proved that Bigfoot exists and have my dead mangled body pictured on the cover of a trash tabloid. I was not prepared mentally to witness any such monstrous phenomenon that night. I was ready to see some ghosts, not catch a glimpse of Oklahoma's Bigfoot. The Creature has been spotted all across the state and to think that I could possibly have spotted this amazing phenomenon continues to overwhelm me.

No matter what part of the state you are in, just make sure you pay attention to what is lurking beyond the road. Take a detour off the main highway and see Oklahoma's mysteries firsthand. Take the time to soak up local culture and mysterious lore. There are many types of roadside phantoms. All across the world there have been reports of ghostly hitchhikers. From the lady in white, the car-jumping man to gruesome creatures, the legends are intriguing. Your children will thank you for it later if you allow them to keep the legends alive to pass on to their children. Just remember, if you see someone walking down the road at sunset, be hesitant before you pick him up. Roadside mysteries do exist and they happen to people just like you.

GRANDMA'S HOUSE

Submitted by Lana Billings

It was right after we moved into my grandmother's old house in Enid in 1990. My grandmother never remodeled the house even though she lived there for over 40 years. She always thought it was perfect just the way it was.

We decided to update the main bathroom. We joked about Grandma getting mad at us as we took the tile and the floor out.

One afternoon, we had been working on the bathroom and decided to take a break. We were relaxing in the living room when a huge gust of wind came down the hallway from the bathroom, flung open the storm door leading outside and then slammed the door shut. We just sat there stunned for a while. I mean, where does a gust of wind come from inside of a house? I knew then that my grandma had gotten mad and left the house. She never bothered us much after that.

Recently, I came home from work one evening. My son Josh's truck was in the driveway so I assumed he was home. As is my habit I hollered, "Hello!" when I walked in the door. I heard Josh's voice reply, "Hello!" I walked through the house to talk to him and to my surprise he was not home. Someone had come over and picked him up. I definitely heard a male voice answer me that night. It kind of made the hair on the back of my neck stand up!

A VERY "TOUCHING" EXPERIENCE

Submitted by Jason Clark

This is a true story of a haunting in a house in Guymon.

I had friends who rented the house for several years. The family reported that it was not uncommon to hear the sound of people running through the house when no one was there. Odd little things would happen, but nothing was seen. The haunting seemed to consist of sounds and small objects being moved or misplaced.

One evening I went over there for dinner. After dinner, most of the family went to the den to watch television. My friend and I headed to the bedroom so we could talk without the interruption of the television. I went into the bedroom as my friend went to use the bathroom. As I entered the room, there was a little girl in a dress. I knew beyond a shadow of a doubt that she was not a living person; she had a kind of misty appearance, but I could see her.

I began to cry, which is not typical of me. My friend came in but she could not see the little girl. At that, the spirit girl went over to my friend and touched her arm. My friend cried out that her arm had suddenly gone numb with cold. Then the ghost girl simply turned away from us and vanished.

We never saw her again.

SURETY ABSTRACT
By Tammy Wilson

A historic building in Enid, Oklahoma, Surety Abstract, has been home to some odd goings on. Most of us remember it as Lambert's, a high-end dress shop, but before it was Lambert's, it was a department store called Herzberg's.

Dennette Ray, owner of Surety Abstract, jokingly made a comment to a long-time Enid attorney that she and her employees thought the building might be haunted. They had witnessed several strange occurrences and were unable to explain them any other way. The attorney thought for a moment and stated he didn't really know why it would be haunted. They finished their business and he returned to his office only to reappear a short time later with an old newspaper article. The attorney showed Ray the article and declared, "You know, it just might be haunted."

The 1956 news article related a tragic story about a woman who was employed by Herzberg's Department Store. Her estranged ex-husband came into the store one afternoon while she was working and demanded that she give him $70 for a dentist visit. She refused and he shot her to death, then shot and killed himself, right there in the store. Ray had been unaware of this story until she saw the article.

The employees at Surety have seen stacks of items knocked off the counter; they have heard unexplained noises and seen people walk by who vanish when they turn to look.

The Eerie Oklahoma team was allowed to conduct an investigation in the historical downtown building and they were not disappointed with what they found. There was a light at the back exit that seemed to flicker and act strangely all night. We asked the owners if that were normal. They assured us it was not. We were sitting on the floor in the area where the murder-suicide took place when one of the members reacted to something moving behind her and touching her. I had also looked up because I thought I saw something, but alas, there was nothing there.

As we wandered around on the main floor of the big building, we heard noises coming from upstairs. It sounded as if someone were moving something heavy, like furniture. I was going toward the stairs to see if the noises were being made by the other part of the group when they came walking up the stairs from the basement. None of us had been upstairs at all!

We have spoken with the owner of the building and will be going back to investigate further. Always wanting to know as much as I can about a location, I interviewed the children of Dick Lambertz, the building's previous owner. His daughter, Brooke Reed, and her brother, Matt Lambertz, stated that as children, they explored every possible nook and cranny of the old building while playing hide-and-seek. They never had any ghostly encounters, but they were spooked by the store mannequins more than once.

Another of Brooke Reed's brothers, Gant Lambertz, is of the opinion that the spirit behind the haunting is that of his father, Dick Lambertz, who was a very popular and jovial man in life.

"This is the large building to the south that Lambert's occupied in its last years of existence, where Dick held an auction one week prior to his passing to 'get all his affairs in order.' This was not the building with the mannequins," he said. "The air conditioner and the elevator always had a squeak, which could explain the noises heard from the first floor. The 'haunting' that could be going on could be all the elder ladies hitting on the handsome Dick Lambertz in the better place that they all now share."

THE COLD ROOM
Submitted by Mark Keefer

In 1999, my brother and I moved into a house in Enid, Oklahoma. We decided that rather than living in two separate apartments, we would pool our resources and move into a decent rental. The house was located on the far southeastern side of town in an average neighborhood. Not long after we moved in, we noticed some very strange occurrences in the house. For example, I had recently spent some time in the hospital and was still off work. One afternoon, as I was lying on the couch, I started hearing a noise. At first, the noise was simply annoying, but it got louder and louder. The noise eventually got so loud that it seemed as if someone was trying to break into the house. Of course, I investigated, but could not find the source of the noise or even a logical cause. At that point, I was just feeling too ill to keep looking, so I went and got my .357 and simply lay back down.

There were plenty of other things that happened in that house to cause me to wonder if it might be haunted. In the master bedroom, there was a rather large walk-in closet. The light switch for the closet was on a wall in the bedroom. This light was constantly coming on when it shouldn't have been. For instance, I would make sure the light was off before I went to bed; otherwise it would have shone under the door and bothered me. There were several times I would wake up in the middle of the night or in the morning and the light was back on. I'm sure someone would try to explain this away as an electrical short or something, but the light switch would be turned to the "on" position. Someone or something was turning it on.

An avid fan of the Austin Powers films, someone had given me a near life-size replica of one of the stars of the movie, Mini-Me. The replica was about a foot and a half tall and was capable of standing on its own. Mini-Me had a spot on a shelf in the living room. However, much like the light switch in the living room, he didn't always stay in one position. I could be watching television, leave the room, come back and Mini-Me would have moved on his shelf. They weren't just slight movements, either. Sometimes, Mini-Me would be facing directly towards me and when he was moved, he would be facing away from me.

However, the most chilling examples of strange occurrences in this particular house were things told to us by children. We had a room in the house that was rarely used. Any time you walked by it, you could noticeably tell a difference in the temperature coming from the room. It was always ice cold - even with the vents shut off. Then, suddenly, it would return to normal and sometimes back to cold. On occasion when my nephew would come to visit us, we would attempt to get him to stay in the room. He flatly refused. He referred to the "little boy" in the room, a little boy who didn't want him in there.

Shortly before I moved out of that house, my girlfriend (later my wife) brought over a child whom she was babysitting. He played for a while in the backyard and then came running in crying. When asked what was wrong he said, "The little boy that lives here doesn't want me here." When pressed, he said that the little boy lived in the shed in the backyard. The shed also was something about the house that was strange: it was always like the room in the house, almost always cool. It could be a hot sunny summer day and you could open that old rusty shed and it would be cool in there, and it was always muddy too. For whatever reason, this shed didn't sit on a slab; it had a dirt floor and the floor was always muddy, so we didn't store anything out there.

I had no problem moving away from that house.

WOODWARD MEMORIAL HOSPITAL
By Tammy Wilson

Woodward was the site of one of the biggest and most destructive tornadoes in Oklahoma history in 1947. There were over one hundred lives lost. It was this tornado that prompted the implementation of the tornado watch system in 1953 that has since saved countless lives.

Witnesses have reported red eyes in the windows, small children that disappear when approached, and people looking out of the windows of the old Woodward Memorial Hospital. In the spring of 2005, it was owned by a family that was not prone to giving into frivolous ghost stories. They eventually came to accept the strange occurrences that took place in the old building in their backyard and even did some investigations of their own, including collecting some EVP.

On May 27, 2005, the Eerie Oklahoma paranormal investigation team, along with two guests from GHOULI (Ghost Haunts of Oklahoma and Urban Legends Investigations), investigated the old Woodward Hospital. The hospital has been closed since around 1950 when a newer and more

Some of the destruction of the terrible Woodward, Oklahoma tornadoes in 1947.

(Courtesy of City of Woodward, Oklahoma)

modern building was erected.

The team sat down with George Pareja, the building's owner at the time, who explained what he had seen and heard. He also played some EVPs that were allegedly taken in the hospital. They then did a

walkthrough as a group to become familiar with the layout of the building.

There was no electricity as the hospital has been closed for many years. George was thoughtful enough to bring in an extension cord, lamp and table. The group broke into teams of two and went to different areas of the building to sit and observe.

Two of the teams were upstairs to separate wings of the hospital. Both teams reported hearing noises like someone walking around at the point where the two wings met in the middle. There were also two teams of two on the main floor, in the area believed to have been the lobby, and the emergency room ambulance bay. Another two-person team was in the

A Night time view of the old Woodward Memorial Hospital

basement. There were several voice recorders and two video cameras, one on a tripod, stationary at the bottom of the main staircase, with another positioned on a small footlocker in the emergency room hallway.

Later, when they analyzed all of the footage, they noticed one of the cameras picked up something odd. About thirty minutes into it there are two thuds and then this wispy, stringy- looking object whizzed by the camera.

The possibility of it being a spider web blowing past was considered, but it moved very quickly and upon rewinding the video, it was not visible on the screen. No one had been down the hall and no one heard the thumps that occurred on the video, although one team was stationed at the other end of the hall and heard noises in that area. In fact, it seemed so clear someone was there that one of the investigators went into the hall and called out and looked around, but there was nothing there.

There was a lot of outside noise and interference, so this investigation did not yield much usable evidence. The building had at least three open exterior doors and numerous broken windows, which allowed the consistently high winds to rush through, creating excessive noise, particularly in the basement. It did add to the spooky atmosphere though! Complicating the matter were the local curiosity-seekers, who produced a great deal of noise outside the hospital that was easily heard through the building's numerous openings. At one point, several teenagers who had entered during the first sit-down session were asked to leave for the time being, but they didn't comply for long.

Is the old Woodward Hospital haunted? A lot of people have witnessed unusual things in the building and other Oklahoma paranormal investigation teams have spent a considerable amount of time there. The hospital has changed owners but apparently the new owners have reported odd things happening to them as well. While the Oklahoma City Ghost Club was there, they had experiences similar to those of the Eerie Oklahoma and GHOULI teams. They would hear voices or noises and would rush to find the source only to be faced with nothing. They witnessed movements that did not appear on their video and heard sounds that were not recorded.

At least one hundred and sixteen lives were lost in the terrible storm of 1947, three of them children who were never identified. The storm tore the community apart and is still listed as the most deadly in Oklahoma history. The front lawn of the hospital became a makeshift morgue as bodies were collected from the surrounding area. As with any hospital, there is the possibility of hauntings because of the loss of life and traumatic things that happened there, but considering the magnitude of the trauma and loss at the Woodward Memorial Hospital, the possibility could very well be even higher than usual.

GHOSTLY ZIPPO
By James Bradley

I've never held a strong belief in the paranormal. But when my grandmother was diagnosed with cancer a few years ago, I revised my point of view after we both found ourselves recipients of a message of hope from a departed loved one, delivered in a startling way. It is a special moment I will never forget.

My grandmother was diagnosed with breast cancer in 2003. It struck everyone hard, since my grandfather had passed away a few years before, after suffering a long agonizing battle with throat cancer. Each day, my grandmother had remained at his side, determined to see him through, an act of courage most in my family could not muster. "Papa" had been a remarkable man to all of us and to see him beaten by a faceless enemy was more than we could bear. So it came as a shock when our "Nanny" was suddenly thrust before the same nemesis.

The doctors scheduled her for surgery several weeks after the cancer was diagnosed. Nanny's fear of the upcoming breast removal plagued her day-to-day activities. She had just turned seventy years old. At that age, the relatively normal act of going "under the knife" posed risks far too numerous to count. It scared her to death. So she withdrew to the shelter of her home and its bittersweet comfort.

Her house was built by Papa in the early 1950s and expanded upon through the nearly thirty-five years of their marriage. It held sweet memories of family Thanksgivings and magical Christmases. Every holiday and season was celebrated with lovingly chosen decorations and scented candles. It truly reflected the theme of Home Sweet Home.

Yet its walls spoke too of their creator's passing. When Papa had been diagnosed as terminally ill, Nanny refused to let him succumb to the inevitable in some strange, cold place. He was too weak to argue with her and surrendered to the hospice of their home. After only a few months his final dignity was ripped away when he could no longer care for itself and became dependant on others.

At first, Nanny became his sole caretaker, refusing anyone else's help. But the reality of caring for every human need of another in addition to her own became too much. Finally, she acquiesced and allowed a nurse to relieve some of the burden.

She was occasionally comforted by family members willing to visit. On some occasions they tempted her with stepping out for dinner or a walk in the sun. She refused every time. The thought of leaving Papa when he lay helpless and racked with pain filled her with guilt. She slept on the couch next to his bed each night and stayed until the end, ignoring pleas to release his hand from her grasp for nearly an hour after his death.

This final act of devotion was rewarded with a suddenly empty house filled with the personal possessions of her husband and best friend, artifacts of a great man's life and passions. It would take nearly three years to pack away the memories of thirty-five years of marriage and remove beloved articles like a pipe tobacco-scented flannel coat last hung by its owner's hand. But the house would always be her home so the family did their best to make it more comfortable for her. One of the ways they did that was to dispose of many of Papa's belongings.

On the afternoon prior to her scheduled surgery date, a friend and I, at the behest of my aunt, agreed to hang a new light fixture in the family room. Shortly after removing the old fixture, I realized that the screws accompanying the new light weren't compatible with the original ceiling kit, preventing me from completing the task. Glancing toward the door leading to the garage, I remembered a large assortment of screws lay stored in old pipe tobacco cans along a workbench where grandfather had tinkered throughout my life. Asking Nanny if I could enter what had become a place off-limits to everyone but she would hit a very sensitive nerve.

Earlier that year, my family had convinced Nanny to let them clean out the two-car garage, one side of which had been Papa's workshop. It was an ordeal for all involved, but one of the most touching moments for me. At some point, Nanny had called and asked me to come over. She wanted me to have Papa's favorite pipe and his tobacco pouch. I was moved by the gesture and was surprised to see that the pipe's bowl was still filled with half smoked tobacco. The pouch too, was still filled. But Papa had always fired up his pipe with a brass Zippo lighter, which was absent from the grouping of gifts.

I asked if I might have the lighter too. Nanny said it hadn't been found and was probably lost or misplaced. The idea of it being gone gave me a pang. Too many memories included Papa in a cocked ball cap with his pipe clenched between his teeth, cupped fingers protecting the flame of the Zippo. Those movements, and the smells that each produced, are among my fondest recollections of Papa. But I was thrilled to have been given the pipe and tobacco pouch. I just regretted that so many other heirlooms had been removed from his garage workshop.

When I explained to Nanny my need for the light fixture screws, she reluctantly allowed me access to the garage, reminding me to leave everything else alone. But when I stepped into Papa's former domain I felt like an intruder. I could only imagine what it must have done to Nanny when so many people helped themselves while clearing out his accumulation of disparate materials.

Glancing up in the rafters, I sought the stacks of electric railroad train boxed sets that had been stored there. Collecting them was Papa's favorite pastime. They were all gone.

Stepping around Nanny's dust-covered car, I passed the dresser drawers where an old stereo once sat tuned into an oldies or occasional country station while Papa tinkered away nearby. Beyond that was a standalone vice grips, where he would let me pretend to build inventions never before seen by man. I smiled at the thought of Papa tightening its clamps around a block of wood that I would soon have sawed, nailed, and glued into a ridiculous something-or-other with any one of the seemingly hundreds of tools available to me throughout the garage. None but the grips remained. The sounds of his tinkering had become only silent memories.

With a sigh, I moved toward the inner sanctum of his former workbench, picked clean months before. The bare bins and empty tool slots reminded me of my loss and how much I missed him.

From the rows of tobacco cans remaining and arranged along the back of the bench, I soon determined which one most likely held the fixture screws I needed. Reaching across the bench I felt a slight tingle. Part of me wanted to say it was related to my feeling of intrusion. But another told me it was something else.

Looking down, I was startled to see a Zippo lighter lying on the bench top. It lay flat, in the middle of the work surface, and out in the open. A small pipe logo on the lower corner of the casing identified it as a pipe lighter. I realized immediately that it was Papa's missing Zippo.

Stepping back, it took me some moments to think about what I was seeing. Looking around I reassured myself that the entire area and most of the garage had been gone through with a fine-toothed comb. There was no way his lighter, lying out in the open on the workbench, could have been overlooked. I distinctly remembered Nanny telling me it had not been found and was thought lost or misplaced. My first instinct was to snatch it up and run into the house showing everyone. But the second told me to quietly let my grandmother know and see what she wanted to do with his final possession.

I spoke to Nanny first and led her into the garage. I could tell being there was having an effect. Her features became slightly pinched, reacting to the difficult environment.

Stepping up to the work bench, I pointed out the lighter. She seemed to stare at it forever and I at her, both of us unsure of what it meant. Soon, however, she reached forward and slowly picked it off the counter top.

"Its warm," I remember hearing her say. She passed it to me and I confirmed that it indeed felt warm to the touch. I was reminded of how it might feel had someone just removed it from their pocket. Handing it back, I watched her eyes mist slightly.

The memories of her friend, lover, and husband seemed to flash across the gaze. Thoughts of the trim fireman of long ago, sweeping a young waitress from her feet by ordering a piece of pie every day at the diner where she worked, just to get to know her better. Of the man who took on the role of father for children not his own after she finally acquiesced and married him. And of the caretaker and provider who never left them without. Of the stoic man who said more in actions than in words.

While looking at her expression, momentarily focused on another time and place, it suddenly occurred to me the Zippo reflected more in its worn case than the face of an old woman. She seemed to will its former owner for a last dance or walk along the boulevard of yesteryear by peering into her reflection with an unusual intensity. It was if she were begging him to stay with her always and be by her side when she needed him most.

For a moment she raised the lighter as if to declare, "You owe me!" or "I need you now. Why didn't you stay? Why?" Then for some reason, she pulled the lid open with her other hand and pushed down against the Zippo's wheel with an aged thumb, daring it to release the ghost of her husband.

An eruption of flint sparks burst the lighter's wick into a large, bright, spectral flame. The intensity and unexpected operation startled her back to the present, forcing her to throw the lighter away. It landed on the bench top back in its original position, leaving us speechless.

Our minds and hearts raced. Did it really just happen? What did it mean? How could it have happened? How did the lighter come to be on the bench to begin with?

I could tell right away that Nanny was really shaken up, but not with fright. We looked at each other for what seemed an eternity, trying to conclude if we had each seen the same thing. From our eyes and expressions, we had.

Embracing, we sobbed and reassured each other for a few minutes. It was the first time we felt elated and free of the sorrow of Papa's passing three years earlier. We knew in unspoken words that he had reached out from another place and confirmed that her soul mate still walked among us. She knew and was comforted, in that brief moment, that his presence would support her through the next day's surgery and beyond.

Picking the Zippo up from the bench once more, she pressed it into my palm and squeezed my hand reassuringly. With brief nods of understanding, we left the garage. Upon entering the house, we shared our experience with my aunt and my friend, neither of whom believed us.

Passing the still-warm lighter to them for examination, I was struck by their first statement. Each of them declared that the casing was cold. My grandmother inspected it again and repeated my own sentiments: the lighter felt warm to the touch, a fact we never seemed to prove to others.

After installing the light fixture, I soon left for home. Upon arriving, I was anxious to inspect the lighter more closely. At the time, I was a pipe smoker like my grandfather before me. My hope was to use the memorable lighter as my own. But try as I might, the lighter wouldn't work, even after dismantling and cleaning the innards and adding lighter fluid to its long-dry packing.

Perplexed, I sent it to Zippo for repair. Within a few weeks I received the lighter back with a note from their company repairman. It stated that the original workings could not be repaired without damaging them and that in no way could they have operated as I had described, in such a state and with lack of fuel. The note went on to say that the lighter fluid would have evaporated long before I had found the lighter, rendering it inert. The Zippo's workings had been replaced with new ones and the originals returned to me in the same package.

I was dumbfounded yet glad to have the lighter in working order. But try as I might, the lighter would not operate. Each time I tried to light my pipe, the flame would sputter and die. Was it a final message from beyond the grave about the dangers of smoking? Whatever the reason, I put my pipe away and quit smoking shortly afterwards.

Looking back, I'm relieved the Zippo had been found and I still remain deeply moved by what appeared to be my grandfather's way of reaching out and letting my Nanny and I know that he was still with us. The day after the strange incident, my grandmother entered surgery, the lighter held in her hand for the duration. No problems ensued and she recovered fully from the ordeal.

Since that fateful afternoon, when I am moved to do so, I gaze upon the small grouping of pipe, pouch, and lighter. I am reminded to be a good man by memories of a great one. When troubled, I may even hold the inert Zippo while sitting in quiet contemplation. Among my thoughts is the love its former owner had for his wife and family and how that same love and presence continues to embrace a select few.

A HAUNT AT THE HOSPITAL

Submitted by Russell White

I used to work in a hospital in Oklahoma City. One night I was walking down one of the back hallways with one of the security guards. The hallway was approximately sixty to seventy-five yards long and from where we were walking it was possible to see all the way to where the hall came out into a surgery waiting room.

I was walking and chatting with the guard, looking down the hall. Now, in this area at that time of night it was semi-dark and everything was locked up. As I looked down the hall, a black human-shaped object appeared from the left side of the waiting room. It was solid black. I saw no features other than what looked like arms extended over the top of it. The thing appeared to be bending back and forth from the waist while turning in circles. Whirling around and around, it seemed to be moving almost in slow motion.

I immediately broke out in goose bumps and said to myself, "I must have been chasing too many ghosts."

The security guard blurted, "Did you see that? Somebody just ran across there."

We hustled down the hall and came to the waiting area where the thing had gone from left to right across my field of vision. Whatever it was had disappeared. The only place it could have gone was to the big glass doors that lead into the outpatient surgery area, which were locked.

The only other thing I noticed was that it was very cold there but in a hospital it's always cold.

THERE'S A MONSTER IN THE CLOSET
Submitted by an Anonymous Website Reader

In Ponca City, there is a house that was probably built around the late 1930s. It is a two-story structure complete with a basement, a frightening apparition and a hideous something that lurked in one of the closets. I spent a large portion of my youth there.

There were two main apparitions that showed themselves to me and my younger sister. I remember that as we went up the stairs, the feeling of unease and dread would begin to build.

If we were lucky, the light would remain on until we reached the upper story. As we reached the end of the stairs, many times we were certain we saw what appeared to be a flaming skull coming from the bathroom. If we weren't lucky then we knew that awaiting us in the bedroom was the ghoul. I still have nightmares about this thing. She stayed mainly in the closet. But it didn't matter to her if you shut the door or not, she would open it. All we could see of her was a decomposing head and hear hideous laughter and carrying on.

There were a few instances of the beds being shaken, electrical disturbances such as lights flickering and the phone ringing with no one on the line. The radio would play by itself. We had water taps that had minds of their own, as well.

The house, being older, would creak, groan, snap, crackle and pop... settling, you know. As a child it amazed me that a house could settle in the exact replication of footsteps on the stairs.

It was a very spooky house. I have considered many times taking a trip back to Ponca, just to knock on the front door and see if it is still haunted.

Was it just an old house with bad electricity and faulty plumbing? Were these the trappings of childhood imaginations? Do two people usually imagine the same horrific things at the same time? It's quite possible, I suppose, but as an adult, it's still unsettling to me. I know now that the house probably wasn't as spooky as it seemed then, but believe it or not, I'm still traumatized and this story is still very scary to me.

EVERYONE KNOWS THE MUSEUM IS HAUNTED!

By Tammy Wilson

It was homecoming weekend 1993 at Northwestern Oklahoma University in Alva, Oklahoma. Normally I went home to Enid on the weekends, but I had helped build the drama club float for the parade and I was in the color guard of the marching band so I had to stay and attend the football game that afternoon. There were few options for entertaining oneself in Alva and I had already exhausted most of them in the two or three months that I had been there. I decided I would check out the Cherokee Strip Museum, as I hadn't done that yet. It was a big brick building that looked like it was pretty old. Upon entering, there was a lady at the front desk and no one else around. As with most museums, the silence was deafening. I started up the stairs as I thought I'd check out the top floor first and work my way down. As I was going up, a friend of mine and her family were coming down, leaving the museum. We exchanged hellos and went on our separate ways. The curator and I were then alone in the quiet museum.

The upper floor was basically a long hallway with rooms on both sides. Deciding that I would start at one end and work my way to the other, I began my long trek down the hall. The first room I went in was done up as an old operating room, tables and all. There were archaic machines that were at one time state-of-the-art life saving devices. It was a little creepy - they looked more like some kind of shiny torture traps. Even so, they were quite intriguing. Across the hall from the operating room was a room done up as an old funeral parlor, complete with an ancient carriage basket just the right size for a body, old embalming paraphernalia: the works. Just the nature of that room made me feel a bit uncomfortable and gave me an unpleasant sense of my own mortality. Against the wall at the end of the hallway, sandwiched between the operating room and the funeral parlor, was an old medical contraption of some sort that had switches and so forth on it. It was not something I was familiar with or could figure out a use for, but it seemed to fit in with all the other aged trappings of illness, death, and decay.

I wandered, looking in every room, seeing all the stuff of a small town museum. I was at the opposite end of the hall from where I started when I heard voices and saw, out of the corner of my eye, some people come up the stairs and enter the upper floor. Turning to see who was there, I saw no one. I assumed they went into one of the rooms at the other end of the hall. Going on about my business of historical enlightenment, I again saw movement, so once more I turned to see what was there. No one. "Hmmm... How puzzling," I thought to myself as I traveled the length of the corridor back toward the operating room, scanning every room on the way, only to find myself completely alone. Then I noticed something very odd indeed - the lights on the machine standing against the wall were lit up. They hadn't been before! In fact, I wasn't entirely sure it had even been plugged in to an electrical outlet. Considering I was obviously the only person on this floor, I was more than a little spooked after hearing voices, seeing people walking around, and lights lighting up on the ancient medical contraption, so I decided to go back downstairs to see if perhaps I had missed something and there were more people down there. It occurred to me that it was possible the voices were simply carrying up the stairs. I went down to the main floor only to find that I was the only visitor in the museum.

After my mysterious afternoon at the museum, I relayed the story to my roommate and she agreed it was indeed very strange. We decided to consult our neighbor, her aunt, as she was a longtime native of the small town. I told her of the voices, the people walking who turned out to not be there, the lights on the old machine, the creepy sensation in the operating room. Her response was, "Yeah. That's the old hospital. Everyone knows it's haunted." Well, maybe not everyone...

I had not lived in Alva long enough to know the local folklore and I had no idea about the history of the old building. The layout made more sense upon learning of its former life as a hospital. Apparently, the operating room equipment was original to the building. Without prior knowledge of the haunting, I could not go with the theory that my mind was playing tricks on me; I was there just to kill some time before a football game.

Later that fall, the drama club to which I belonged decided to have their Halloween party at the museum one crisp night in October. Needless to say, I was more than a little ambivalent when they shut off the lights and herded us up the stairs by flashlight to the old operating room...

SOMEONE TO WATCH OVER ME?

Submitted by Samara Stephenson

Back in the 1980s I experienced a couple of situations, both related to the Arkansas River, both of which were somewhat inexplicable.

The first one happened in broad daylight on the bridge at 23rd Street as it crosses the Arkansas River. I was despondent and had decided to make my own hole in the river. I stood at the outlook, watching the water get sucked under the Ogee Weir.

I had just put my foot up on the bench so that I could climb up on the ledge in order to finish my thoughts and myself, (that bench is no longer there) when someone hollered, "Hey!"

I turned around and coming from the middle of the bridge was a man in a trench coat, a really scruffy man, dirty, and smelly. At first I was afraid that he planned to harm me, and then I got tickled at myself because I realized I was planning exactly the same thing, so this was possibly not a bad thing.

The man approached me, saying nothing, but holding out a small pamphlet. "Oh, great!" I thought to myself, "He wants money for his church!" But I took the paper anyway. As I expected there were praying hands drawn on the front. I opened it and instead of the rant and ballyhoo I expected inside, the message was very simple. It said merely: "Jesus loves you." That was it. So, I turned it over to see what organization had printed it. There was nothing on the back. I looked up, surprised, to speak with the man but he was gone. He was not on the bridge anywhere. It is quite a distance to that outcropping, but he was not there. I had only glanced away long enough to read those three words. The whole thing shook me to my core, and I decided, whatever the situation, that day was not my day to die. I should note that I had been raised Christian, but had not been involved in that religion for a period of time. That had been my only spiritual connection.

The second situation also happened on the Arkansas River. I was living in a gross apartment near downtown. I had neighbors living above me: a man, his wife and teen-aged daughter. Before I came to live there, I had spent the previous twelve years of my life with an abusive man. One night, the neighbors were having a fight. I could hear the man screaming at his wife and her cries of anguish. It got louder and more intense. Furniture was being tossed about. I was starting to get very upset. I asked my roommate if we should call the police and was advised against it, as it would make an enemy of the man.

I continued to get more and more anguished, reliving all those abusive occasions in my own life. I could not take the sounds any more and ran away from the apartment. It was approximately two or three in the morning. I drove to the river and pulled into a parking lot, got out of my car and ran away to a big old elm on the bank. It was dark and quiet there, and I started crying.

After a while, a man came over to my tree. He seemed oddly familiar, wearing a trench coat and not especially clean. He knelt down beside me and asked what was wrong. I told him what had happened. He remained there, quiet for a while longer while I continued to cry. He just stayed with me as I calmed down. Eventually, he looked around and said that I might want to go on back to the apartment. He said he was sure the ruckus was over and that it was not safe for me to stay any longer at the river. He was so calm and peaceful and I felt reassured by his words. I followed his advice and went home. Sure enough, all was calm upstairs and the situation never occurred again.

THE PASSENGER
Submitted by David McCoy

Mid-October in Oklahoma presents a breathtaking panorama of colors with the diverse foliage across the landscape, the crisp in the air, and the chill of early frost. There was nothing unusual about this particular day.

Being a freight terminal manager brings many responsibilities, one of which is opening the terminal for customers by 7:00 a.m. six days a week. The daily routine required being up and ready to travel the seventy miles from Enid to Ponca City. Just as in the previous six months, the morning was rolling along on schedule. Now, as many times before, my dad, Curtis McCoy, rode along in the passenger seat. We discussed family and past and future activities. We talked about our gun-fighting days at the Frontier City amusement park and many things to come. Time passed quickly and before I knew it Ponca City was on the horizon. The morning's travel had come to a close. After arriving at the terminal, I unlocked the gate and returned to my car only to find I was alone. Suddenly I realized I must have been alone the entire trip, or was I...?

You see, my Dad had passed away at home three weeks prior to that day of a massive heart attack. Since then he has chosen several times to visit and I welcome every opportunity to converse with him.

SPIRITS OF SAPULPA

Submitted by an Anonymous Reader

I live in Sapulpa, Oklahoma. My husband and I have lived in an apartment there for the last three years.

My daughter and her best friend noticed the strange happenings way before I did: doors opening for no reason, her CDs sliding across the kitchen floor, lights flickering on and off... I always gave her an explanation for these things, but I knew deep down it was only to calm her fears. I have had unexplained things happen before my eyes in the past and knew in my gut that what was causing them was not of this world.

When my daughter was old enough to move out and live on her own, I started to experience things myself. I had heard the stories from the neighbor across the breezeway of how no one ever seemed to live in my apartment longer than a few months because of the strange things that went on. I was the longest to ever live here.

One night I was at my computer doing my work - I am a genealogist - when I saw something out of the corner of my eye move past my office door. I was the only one home and the apartment was dark except for a few nightlights and the lamp on my desk. I shrugged it off thinking it was nothing but it happened again about twenty minutes later.

There were no windows open anywhere, yet I felt as if something or someone walked past as cool air breezed by me. I again shrugged it off since I was tired and had put in a very long day and evening working.

About a week or so later the same thing happened, but with a different outcome. When I saw whatever it was go by my office door, I turned to look and caught a glimpse of the back of a woman. Surprised, I got up and went to the door and looked down the hallway toward the kitchen/living room but there was nothing there. I was alone in the apartment.

The next day around 1:30 p.m. I was again working and happened to turn and look toward the hall and there she was. She never glanced at me as she walked by; it was as if I were not even there to her. She wore mid- to late-1800s-style clothing, a pioneer-looking dress with an apron, and a bonnet that was tied around her neck and hanging down her back. She looked as if she were carrying something in her arms, sheets or towels or something. She walked by as if she were headed to put these things away, maybe the wash she had done that morning, I do not know, but that is the impression I got.

Now, the really interesting thing happened later that night. As usual, I

was working at the computer. I saw her again, only it seemed she was carrying something else, and this time when she passed by there was a young girl who followed her dressed basically the same as the older woman. The girl was carrying a bucket and whatever was in it must have been heavy because she was bent over somewhat and holding onto the handle with both hands, as if she were being very careful not to spill the contents. Behind the young girl walked an older man. He was wearing a long-sleeved shirt and cover-alls and sported an old beat-up hat on his head. He looked dirty and tired and was carrying a harness. They were all headed toward the master bedroom.

About ten minutes later the younger girl walked past alone but it seemed the bucket she carried was empty as she now carried it with ease. Never once did any of them acknowledge that I was there. It was as if they were going about their daily and evening chores as usual in a time far away from where I existed.

I had a dog at the time and I know she was seeing the same things as I was because she lay under my desk all the time when I was working. I believe that animals can sense the supernatural and I take heed when they act strangely. There had been other times when she seemed scared and would hide or growl and bark at nothing, or what appeared to be nothing, but this time my dog watched them pass by one by one and never uttered a sound. It was as if they were a common thing for her to see.

I have seen these people on two other occasions but mostly I feel their presence more than anything. They have never once tried to scare me or make me leave. I feel they are friendly and I am not frightened in any way. I have seen and felt a lot worse in my life.

I have gotten a new dog as my other passed away and my new little dog has done the same things as her predecessor. One night she was sitting on my lap and staring into the kitchen while we were in the living room watching TV. She gazed into the kitchen for at least five minutes but never made a noise. At one point she wagged her tail.

I hope that my story doesn't seem too outrageous to you, but what I have shared is the truth. My mother says I have a sensitive side to me in that I can feel and see things easily and because of this I have a very open mind to things on matters that can't be easily explained. After all, I did see my grandmother on the day she died. She was in Coffeyville, Kansas, and I was in Pryor, Oklahoma. That was back in 1969 when I was in the seventh grade. I also saw my grandfather a week after he was buried. He gave me a message to give to my mother. I had no idea what the message meant but my mother did and she cried.

Follow up to Sapulpa Story
I had posted this story on the Eerie Oklahoma website and I received the following from someone connected to the story about the apartment in

Sapulpa:

I wanted to comment on the story from Sapulpa. Please excuse me if I seem to ramble, but I am very surprised. I am almost a hundred percent positive that was written by a lady named Jo who lived in the Southern Hills Apartments.

I was her daughter's best friend at the time. I would like to know how she got to "see" the ghosts and we only experienced phenomenon! If that is her, I'm crushed to hear the dog died and glad that she finally got married.

Anyway, this is what happened inside the apartment: I had given her daughter a small stuffed bear for her birthday. If you squeezed it, it would say something about being your special friend. We spent a lot of time in her room, and I started noticing that the bear would sway and turn very slowly and look straight at one of us, usually me. If you moved, it moved. There were no open windows, doors, or even a vent blowing. We brushed it off as our imaginations.

Then the CD player started to skip, especially on certain songs and at different points in the song. Sometimes the player would just shut off. That was all that happened for a couple of weeks or so.

We never took any of this seriously until one specific night. Her mother was out of town and we had spent hours at the computer. I was bored, but she was hooked on the Internet so I just hung out with her and made the best of it. We'd had worse trouble than before with the player. We needed to go to the bathroom at about the same time, so I went to her mother's bathroom and she was right behind me as she went to hers. I heard her door shut. I came back to the kitchen and the CDs had been moved to the floor and placed in a specific pattern. This, I hate to say, scared me more than it surprised me. So I yelled to my friend to see if she had done it, and when she came in she was as surprised as I was.

We placed the CDs about three inches away from the corner of the desk then went back to the computer. A few minutes later something struck the stack of CDs and sent them flying across the room.

We went outside and walked around for a while because that shook us up a bit. After that, when we tried to light our cigarettes, something cold would go by and put out our lighters.

A couple of days after that my friend was cooking and left the room. When she returned, something had taken the potholders out of the drawer, leaving the drawer open, and flung the potholders all over the kitchen. Subsequently, there was still some trouble with CDs, the player, and the bear, but after a couple of weeks it stopped just as suddenly as it started.

I never thought Jo believed us, but if that's her writing the story, I feel better knowing we weren't alone in the experience.

BRICKTOWN BANSHEES
By Tonya Hacker

As you pass through the heart of Oklahoma City, you will also pass through one of the most historic regions in our state. Bricktown, now known as Oklahoma City's entertainment district, is one of the state's most cherished achievements. The streets are lined with cobblestone bricks and the rustic architecture still holds the original charm of yesteryear. Partygoers are drawn to Bricktown's nightlife but some say once the trendy clubs and gourmet restaurants close for the evening, Bricktown takes on a life of its own. There are many tales held within its walls that make Bricktown what it is today. Most buildings are on the cusp of their hundred-year anniversaries. As the district grows, the ghostly tales of Bricktown are finally gaining recognition.

I have become used to hearing rumors about supernatural goings-on from former employees in the Bricktown area since I became a paranormal investigator. I have always had a fondness for that part of the city, mainly because it is a piece of Oklahoma history that actually survived the urban renewal demolitions of the 1980s. As buildings came down all across the metro area, Bricktown remained untouched while the district was in the early stages of being brought back to life by city officials.

Growing up, I was taught not to venture to "the other side of the tracks" while visiting downtown. For years a number of the buildings were abandoned and the homeless flocked to the former warehouse district for temporary shelter. Also during that time, the crack cocaine epidemic was in full force and many drug users would seek refuge within some of the abandoned structures. Bricktown was not a desirable part of downtown for many years, but little did we know that it would eventually prosper and become what it is today: a growing metropolis of clubs, fine dining, and entertainment hot spots.

TapWerks Ale House & Café is one of Bricktown's veteran businesses. Opening in 1999, the owner was not aware of much of the history of the building, but he states that as time goes by he is learning more. It is a four-story structure, complete with a full basement. Each floor has around 4,800 square feet of space. Built in 1912, the building started out as a mattress factory. It provided much-needed work for Oklahomans in the earlier days of the city. The factory survived the Depression and employed hundreds of workers over the years. Walking into the building today you can sense the

Bricktown in Oklahoma City

feeling that it was a place of hard work and virtue. It's a sad fact of history that factory work in Oklahoma sometimes was a deadly trade. Being exposed to boiling summer heat and harsh winters, workers would sometimes perish while on the job. Hazardous working conditions contributed to factory deaths during the early years.

Over time the building was sold and new businesses utilized the massive space. At one stage of its existence, when it was an industrial site; the building housed a chicken hatchery supply company. The last commerce in the building before Bricktown underwent its metamorphosis was a short-lived architectural antique store, but by then the industrial area had started to decline, and eventually the building sat deserted for many years.

After an extensive eight-month restoration, including all new plumbing, electrical wiring, and of course, heating and air conditioning, TapWerks opened its doors to the public. The owner, along with a few others, had high hopes for the newly restored Bricktown district. It wasn't until the business had been up and running for a while that ghostly events started taking place. Even though the paranormal occurrences are subtle, they are a constant reminder of long-ago life in and around the building. More unexplainable personal accounts are popping up every day.

TapWerks' motto is "Where the REAL beers are!" but with some of the paranormal reports coming out of the old building, the ale house can possibly lay claim to being "Where the real GHOSTS are!" In a single night, over one thousand customers may pass through the doors, but when the visitors are gone and the music is turned down is when the building truly comes to life, or so some witnesses declare. Over the years a handful of employees who were spooked enough have spoken out after their ghostly encounters. Most commonly occurrences happen while bar staff or managers are closing up for the evening.

An errand down into the basement has been known to quickly bring staff running up the stairs in fright. The basement is one of the creepier places in the building. Local lore has it there was once a concealed speakeasy in the underground room. Some reports state that during the days of Prohibition the basement was a sanctuary for working men to come and grab a cold drink before heading home. The old front door leading into the basement is in clear view of Sheridan Avenue. The ramped entrance is alleged to have allowed men to lead their horses into the saloon, to keep traffic to a minimum, and of course to help keep the presence of the speakeasy under wraps.

Throughout Oklahoma's history, police constantly raided areas that served alcohol illegally and unfortunately casualties sometimes happened. Employees have reported that while in the basement they have heard footsteps coming from the main bar area upstairs, sounding as if someone were wearing boots. After running upstairs they would find themselves alone and realize that none of the staff were in the building with them. Granted, the old building has its share of creaks and knocks, but some employees would argue that it is not the building's age causing the noises, but rather something paranormal. The sense of being watched, of seeing figures flit past out of the corner of one's eye, sounds of footsteps, and the occasional cold spot are common within the old walls of TapWerks. The possibility that maybe some of the working men of yesterday are still dropping by for a cold beer or stiff drink after work is a frequent source of conversation among the staff and some of the customers. The staff and management don't often speak publicly about the odd things that happen between the historic building's old brick walls, but they're aware that something out of the ordinary seems to be going on. Although they suspect that "last call" has yet to happen in the basement's former speakeasy, they are still sometimes taken aback when the past makes its presence known.

I have had my fair share of unexplainable moments during my own ghostly research, but some of the most memorable moments were those when I was simply caught off guard. It is standard for ghost hunters to always be on the lookout for locations that may be the future mother lode of paranormal research. But sometimes it is the ghosts who choose when to contact us, and as a fearless ghost hunter I quickly learned that I have no control over the other side. About six years ago I was employed in one of the historical buildings directly on the canal that runs through Bricktown. Hired as a service manager of a small ice cream shop, my main goal was to get the store open and ready for the summertime rush. Needless to say, during the colder months I spent most days in solitude. My first realization that something was out of the ordinary with the building was when I was doing the mundane chore of floor mopping. Having white tile, it was a continuous task to keep the floors clean in the shop. While mopping, nothing was out of the ordinary but as I made my way around the front counter, I stood peering over the wet and glistening floor and I remember thinking how I wished it would stay looking like that. Out of nowhere, I heard a man's voice directly behind me say approvingly, "Looks good!" The hairs on the back of my neck stood on end as I slowly turned around to see who was there. Of course I was alone. I quickly put the mop down and headed out the side door wanting only to get out, and get out fast. Once outside I started to think that the voice I had heard came from upstairs. A local chain restaurant was directly on top of my little shop. I headed up the elevator only to find that the cook staff had yet to arrive and all was quiet on the floors above me. I will admit it took me a while to build up the courage to enter the ice cream parlor again, but I finally shook it off and went back to work. At this point in my life I was a devoted ghost hunter, but nothing had prepared me for witnessing a paranormal event while at work.

    A few weeks went by and the owners brought in a batch of decorations to hang on the walls of the store. It was a daunting task as the walls were made of brick. I was not sure how successful I would be in hanging vintage metal trays on the aged walls. I decided to utilize industrial strength Velcro for this mission. The next day, Velcro in hand, I committed the morning to hanging up the trays. I started carefully placing the Velcro strips on the wall. Once the strips were on I had learned that it was not easy to pull them down if I were to hang the trays crooked. After spending the entire morning measuring, cutting the Velcro pieces and strategically placing the vintage decorations on the walls I headed to the back office. The moment I had turned around and taken a couple of steps, a tremendously loud noise came from the parlor. It sounded as if a car had plunged through the front windows. It scared me to the point that I ducked down and sheltered my head. I quickly turned around and went back to see what had just happened. Passing the counter I slowly entered the parlor and then I was shocked to realize that all of the trays were on the floor with the Velcro still attached. As frightful as the noise was, they had to have all fallen simultaneously, with a thunderous crash of metal hitting ceramic tile.

    Upon closer inspection I realized the only way to get the trays down was to pull them off using a lot of muscle. I was spooked and I headed outside to collect my bearings. An hour or so later I entered the parlor again. I had come to the conclusion that whatever was there did not like the decorations. The thought of a ghost finally crossed my mind and I set out to strike a deal with whoever may have been in the building with me. I told the unseen specter that I could lose my job if I did not decorate according to my boss' liking and that my career was on the line. I hastily hung the trays back up and asked that he not touch them anymore. This agreement I assumed was accepted. After that point a few loud bangs of falling metal occurred at very random moments, but nothing as extreme as what I had observed that day.

As the summer months started to approach I was instructed to hire a small staff. I kept the haunting tales to myself because I did not want to scare anyone away. More strange occurrences began to take place and my employees started to witness sporadic paranormal events. I had hired a couple of teenagers to assist with the busy season. Being youngsters, I took advantage of my managerial position and assigned them the less-pleasant tasks, such as taking out the garbage. The old building has no back door. To take out the trash one would have to go through a dark vacant area to an old decrepit freight elevator. It seemed to me the path to the garbage drop had all the trappings of a set from a horror movie. It had all the spooky elements including a creepy wooden door that was the only shield between life and death in the event of an attack. I had a few occasions where I had the sense of being followed and the occasional footsteps rising up behind me so needless to say I didn't mind delegating the task of taking out the trash. The teens would on occasion come running into the shop after dropping off the trash, faces white and trembling with fear. I would always ask them what had happened and in a vague fashion they would tell me about their experiences by the old freight elevator. They all reported the same types of things I had witnessed. Taking the high road, I advised them it was their imagination playing tricks on them, besides I didn't want to go back there, either.

As the season kicked off I hired an assistant manager to help out. She typically worked the evenings to close the shop. There were several occasions where I had to stay late as people flocked in after a ball game. Preparing for a busy evening, she came in early, around 2:00 p.m. We started getting ready for the night in the preparation area of the restaurant. One time, while we were working, we both noticed a man in a red shirt waiting at the counter. We yelled out to him that we would be right there to assist him. I turned to wash my hands and my assistant headed to the front counter. When I arrived she said nobody was there and asked where he could have gone. In the shop there were only two ways out. The front door facing the canal had a bell on it and we did not hear the bell ring. The side doors at that time only led to the main elevator area. I raced out the front door to see where the man in red had gone and she headed to the elevator only to realize the elevators were not moving, and hadn't moved. We both returned to the parlor and talked about how there was no one fitting the man's description in sight. We realized on the spot that the man did not leave through the doors or the elevator. It was impossible for him to just vanish, we thought. But after a few moments we came to the conclusion that we had just seen a full-blown apparition.

The assistant manager began to tell me more about some of the strange things that had happened to her while working the night shift. I was happy to have someone with whom to share my personal eerie experiences. It was evident that the old building had an unearthly inhabitant. It is a rare event for two people to see the same apparition at the same time. The question was, who was this man and why was he so adamant about making his existence known to us?

About a year after the shop closed down, new occupants leased the space to open a similar establishment. The shop is family-owned and operated and they proudly serve the best desserts and cappuccino in Bricktown. One day while visiting Bricktown with my children, we stopped in for a quick treat and to check out the new establishment. Entering the shop I noticed not much had changed and the memories came flooding back to me. While ordering, I boldly asked the owner if anything "strange" ever happened. He smiled and said I needed to speak to his wife. We waited around for the customers to leave them he and his wife started to tell us some of their ghostly encounters in the building. It was music to my ears as they shared similar paranormal events to those I had witnessed. It helped validate a lot of what my fellow employees and I had experienced while working in the shop. We both identified that yes, there was a haunting in the vicinity.

The owners of The Orchard Café have since moved out of the original shop but not far --just a few feet away from the side door to the elevators. The strange occurrences did not cease after the move. Having young daughters working for them, the owners started to experience more examples of paranormal activity. One day, while working behind the counter, one of the owner's daughters was on the telephone. Suddenly her phone was swept away from her hand, landing on the floor. The event frightened her so much that she instantly told her parents what had happened. The owners are rather level=headed when it comes to supernatural claims and they believed their daughter to be telling the truth. She was not one to exaggerate or embellish such things.

The paranormal events did not stop there. Everyone on the canal level was aware of a presence by the old freight elevator. Almost everyone who used the elevator reported the same phenomena: from feelings of an invisible presence to hearing phantom footsteps, not to mention the occasional brush on the shoulder or back from behind and the pockets of extreme cold. As more people entered the building it seemed the ghostly activity became more frequent. The ghostly inhabitants were not discussed much because nobody really understood by whom or why the building was haunted.

A clue to the haunting was soon to be discovered when workers cleaned out the building's upper floors. There were rumors of physical proof confirming that many people died while working in the factories. A bulky wooden door inscribed with the names of workers who had died, along with (in some cases) their dates of death, was said to have existed, but no one had seen it in quite some time. The new owners discovered this door in a very odd way that still has a lot of people perplexed.

The building has a large working elevator with glass windows surrounding the elevator shaft. Travelling upwards, the windows give riders a nice view of the canal. The top floor is home to a private office that is also surrounded by glass. One day, seemingly out of nowhere, large pieces of glass tumbled down into the Orchard Café's dining room. Being early in the morning not many people were in the area. The owners ran to see where the glass was coming from. They could see atop the elevator shaft where the glass had shattered. It was strange because nobody was up there and there were no sounds of gunshots or anything else that could have made the glass break. The glass was quickly cleaned up and replaced.

The operators of the café went on with business as usual until they took the debris to the dumpsters in the alley. In one of the containers, the owner noticed a large wooden door that someone had thrown away. The door was cut into several pieces but as he looked closer he realized that he was seeing the infamous door. He quickly made arrangements to get the door out of the dumpster and salvaged the door that nearly disappeared forever. As he inspected the pieces he realized that the rumors were true; the door was full of names and dates of men who worked and died within the factory walls. The door was installed in a place of honor near the back area of the café and it has been there ever since.

Some say the building's ghostly inhabitants caused the glass to shatter in order to rescue the door that is such an important piece of Bricktown's haunting history. Others claim it was strictly coincidence. No matter what you believe, the shop owners strongly feel this was indeed a serendipitous moment that uncovered an important piece of Oklahoma history. The forgotten names live on and are proudly displayed today. Recently a Native American artist held a small showing of his work in the area of the door. He was drawn to the door and stated to the Orchard's owner, "The men here want to know why do you care now when nobody cared then? They want to thank you".

No matter where you are in Bricktown, always keep your guard up while walking the streets. Stepping into the old buildings can give you an uneasy feeling or even a strong sensation of how hard people actually worked back in the early years of Oklahoma City. Perhaps you will be reminded of the desolate years before the district was restored. Before you enter into today's entertainment district I would like to invite you to take a moment and respect the history behind each establishment. Every building has a past and every brick has a story. From historical battles that were fought on the grounds before statehood to the dedicated workers who made Oklahoma what it is today, it is vital to keep the past in mind. Value the past because you may never know when yesterday will jump out at you.

A HOUSE IN GARBER
By Anna Groom

We used to live in a three-story house in Garber, Oklahoma, right on Main Street. The house was so big with so many rooms that we could have a different bedroom every week if we wanted. After living there for some time, we learned that the house had once been a hospital back in the town's early days. Many odd things happened in that house to several different members of my family.

Every night when I would be sleeping, I would be awakened by the sound of someone running down the halls. I would get scared and run to my mom's room. After that, I wouldn't hear it again for the rest of the night. This literally happened every night.

One day, my aunt and I were cleaning up her room and my mom called to us and told us to come downstairs. When we got there, my grandma told us that my mom had come downstairs, her face white as snow, and told her that when my aunt and I walked to her to get a blanket (she was folding blankets in the upstairs hall), my aunt walked through a man. My mom said that he had black hair and red eyes and when she walked through him he reached up and grabbed her hair and appeared to yank off her head! He then put his finger to his lips as if to say, "Shh."

Aside from this sighting of the black-haired man, there was another time my aunt (head still intact) was upstairs on the third floor and she turned and saw an old man with white hair.

By this time, we all got scared of the house and we started to sleep downstairs. There were two bathrooms, two kitchens, and two dining rooms. We generally only used the left side of the house but we slept in the right-side dining room - all of us except my grandma and grandpa. They slept on the left side downstairs in a side bedroom. My youngest brother was two years old at the time and he would amuse himself by running back and forth in front of the stairs to my grandma's room and back to my mom's bed. He would do this every night, but one night he was running past the stairs and happened to look up and started screaming. My mom and grandma rushed to him, both getting to him at the same time. They said all the color was drained from his face. No one knows what he saw, but he never ran back and forth anymore.

On yet another night I was sleeping in my grandma's bed when I felt someone run their fingers through my hair and rub the top of my head. I was alone. My grandpa said he heard babies cry almost every night.

It's likely the things we saw and heard were related to the fact the house used to be a hospital. Whether they meant us any harm or not was unknown, but they were unsettling all the same. My family currently lives in a house in Enid where there are also uncanny things taking place, but that's another story. The history of the home is being investigated at the time of this writing and already some interesting developments have occurred. Are some of us just more apt than others to see these things? Or did we just get lucky and live in two haunted houses?

THE OLD FARMHOUSE

Submitted by an Anonymous Reader

I grew up in the small town of Thomas in western Oklahoma, nineteen miles north of Weatherford.

My cousins and I used to play hide and seek in the summer time like most kids did. The year this happened it was the summer of 1979 and I was about nine years old. There was a wheat field about the size of a city block across the street to the north of our house. On the north side of the field was an old abandoned two-story house that was mostly burned and collapsed. There was nothing really unusual about this old house until this particular summer.

It had seemed that we were being watched all summer long from someone or something in that house. We had begun playing chicken and daring each other to see who would get the closet to the house and eventually touch it. Since all of us felt that we were being watched from inside the house, it made playing chicken that much scarier. After the farmers had harvested the wheat field we would run up and slap the house and run back.

Usually we had an aunt or uncle sitting outside keeping an eye on us, but not this night. We had all taken our turn at slapping the house and then for some reason we all got scared at the same time. We sat down in a group and all started screaming and crying!

Something came out of the house laughing and walking towards us. It appeared to be a man wearing a trench coat and a hat. He wasn't exactly walking as much as he was floating; his feet were about a foot and a half off the ground.

Well, our grandmother heard the commotion and so did one of our uncles. As they came out, my uncle started yelling and cussing at it and my grandmother was waving a broom at it. They got to us just as it was opening up its trench coat.

This man was all black. Like a shadow is the best I can describe it. As he opened up his coat I could see stars through him, sort of like being out at night and looking at the stars through sunglasses. Coat spread open like a sail, he flew over us and over the street light we were sitting under and then over my grandmother's house and it was over.

MURDER THREE TIMES
By Tammy Wilson

The source of this story is a history of the Enid Police Department that was compiled by, Stephanie Galusha, the wife of a longtime member of the police force, Captain Robert Galusha (Retired). This is my version of the story.

Oddly enough, another obscure piece of Enid's bizarre history rests right outside the Surety Abstract Building, the subject of an earlier story in this collection. The city of Enid is over one hundred years old, older than the state itself. In all that time, only three police officers have ever died in the line of duty.

E.C. Marshall came to Enid when the Cherokee Strip was opened and he became the City Marshal.

J.L. Isenberg was the owner of the *Enid Daily Wave*, a decidedly Democratic newspaper. R.W. Patterson, registrar of the United States Land Office, was also known to be a Democrat; however, the business of the land office went not to the *Daily Wave* but to a newspaper called the *Tribune-Democrat*. This angered Isenberg a great deal and he set out to sully Patterson's reputation by printing unflattering stories about him. As time progressed, the articles became more and more inflammatory and Patterson finally got fed up.

On June 26, 1895, Patterson sought out Isenberg, intending to settle the issue once and for all. The two men met at the corner of Grand and Broadway and commenced to scuffle. Gunshots rang out - Patterson had shot at Isenberg, but missed. Isenberg ran to the safety of a nearby store and Patterson pursued him.

Marshall Williams arrived on the scene and tried to stop Patterson, but in his fury, Patterson turned his gun on Williams, wounding him horribly. Despite being seriously injured Williams charged after Patterson and shot him in the temple, killing him instantly. Williams died shortly thereafter.

Isenberg was never harmed, though two men died because of his actions. He ended up eventually leaving Enid and moving to California.

Nearly eleven years later, Marshal Thomas Radford had become the one to enforce the local law. Being fairly strict, he'd managed to alienate a man named John Cannon.

Now, John Cannon was no stranger to law enforcement, but not in the way one would think: he had once been the county jailer. There was a particular woman of ill repute who spent an inordinate amount of time in jail because of her occupation. Cannon fell in love with her and the two of them were married and opened a rooming house together. Not surprisingly, the rooming house garnered the reputation of being a brothel and the police looked in on them quite a bit.

Cannon had been heard making threats about killing Marshal Radford, but Radford's next plan set the deed in motion. Radford was not happy with Cannon's "business" and had it shut down and forced the tenants out. Cannon then attempted to re-open across the street by renting rooms at the Coney Island Saloon. Radford got wind of this and forbade the owner to rent to Cannon. Cannon was furious and set out to get even.

Vintage postcard of West Randolph Street in downtown Enid

Marshall Radford was warming himself at the radiator and talking with a friend in the Anheuser Busch Building at the corner of Grand and Broadway when Cannon entered the bar, walked up to Radford, and shot him. Radford was shot two more times before he finally collapsed on the sidewalk outside. He died some thirty minutes later, never having regained consciousness after the last bullet hit him in the head.

Cannon was arrested and placed in the Grant County Jail due to the fact that the citizens of Enid would be outraged and possibly moved to violence by the death of one of the best law men they'd had to date.

On a hot July night in 1936, a local tavern owner and former police officer, Jim O'Neal, had gotten word that his bar was about to be robbed, so he was being extra watchful of all who entered his establishment.

A man had come in and was seated at one of the booths having a beer. Two women were waiting outside and he motioned for them to come in. After some time, O'Neal felt confident that he had seen this man in some pictures, so he summoned the local authorities.

Officer Cal Palmer and another officer arrived and they approached the man, asking him to come with them. The man asked to finish his beer. As he chugged the last gulps, he sat the empty stein on the table and as he did so, produced a gun he'd hidden next to him and opened fire. Palmer was killed instantly. The other officer, Ralph Knarr, recovered and later became chief of police. An innocent bystander was wounded as well.

The shooter fled the bar and ran down an alley where he jumped into a car occupied by Fred Caldwell and Dr. LD Huff. The gunman directed them drive and Caldwell proceeded forward until he saw police officers coming at them with their guns drawn. Then he and Huff opened their doors and bailed out, leaving the shooter alone in the car.

Officers converged upon the man and he jumped out of the car and hid behind it. A fatal shot to the head finally took him down. The man was traced to a local hotel where he had been staying with another man for some time. Police captured the second man, Donald Reeder, and learned that the shooter's name was Lawrence DeVol and that he had been the triggerman for the notorious Karpis-Barker Gang. Sixteen people had escaped from the St. Peter, Minnesota, Hospital for the Criminally Insane and Reeder, DeVol, and one other man had been the last of them to evade apprehension. Reeder was returned to Kansas where he was wanted for bank robbery.

It's not all that unusual for police officers to be killed in the line of duty and luckily Enid has lost only three, but the twist to this story is that they all three died on the same corner - the corner of Grand and Broadway. The corner has since become a bit of a superstition amongst the Enid Police Department and it might be wise for you, too, to take a little extra care traveling that route.

A LOST FRIEND, GHOST TRACKS, AND A SPOOK IN THE NIGHT

By Shirley McCoy and Tammy Wilson

My husband's family had owned lake property in Longdale, Oklahoma, for decades. As they became older and developed health problems they seldom used it any longer.

Aunt Jeane's place was burned down by vandals, and David and I had gone to clean up the aftermath. We had worked about sixteen hours that day and collapsed in exhaustion onto the couches in our cabin, which was on the connecting property.

Within no time we were both asleep. Late that night I awoke to the panting breath of a dog on my face and could feel the weight of his paws on the cushion. I murmured something and felt it jump over me and off the other end of the sofa. I heard his footfalls on the hardwood floor as he headed for the door and back outside. As I lay there for a moment I suddenly realized the door was shut and locked, there was no way anything could come or go. Suddenly I was frozen in fear and couldn't get up to wake David.

I kept whispering his name and praying he would hear me and wake. In what seemed an eternity he finally awoke and turned on the lights. When I revealed what had just happened he told me about Corporal, the previous owner's dog. Corporal had been a pal to David and the other lake kids as they explored the woods and fished in the lake. When they barbecued, the scraps were always saved for him. However Corporal had gone into a decline and died upon the passing of his owner.

Perhaps Corporal had returned looking for a new master.

One summer while staying at this same cabin, I was awakened in the night by the rumble of a train and a train whistle. The next morning I commented that I would have slept better had it not been for that blasted train.

My dad took me out behind the cabin a ways to show me the abandoned train tracks that had not been used in several years.

Several years later, after I was grown and had a family of my own and my parents had sold the lake cabin to some friends, my girlfriend, my younger sister, and I decided to take our kids to the cabin for a weekend getaway.

We stocked up on snacks and popcorn and had a fire going in the fireplace as we watched movies and chatted about girl stuff.

My sister and I were sitting together on one couch along the wall and my friend was sitting on another couch that made an "L" shape with the one we were on. The area behind that couch was open, with the kitchen behind it as well as the bathroom. My sister and I both looked up, thinking one of the kids was up and coming to the bathroom. We both clearly saw someone. But there was no one there. We didn't mention it at first, but then nerves finally got the best of us and we talked about it. My friend was terrified and refused to move from that spot for the rest of the night. It was spooky indeed.

The cabin is no longer in our family, but I would be interested to know whether anyone else has had experiences there. That area is rich in Native American culture and there are several paranormal stories about the Canton Lake area, so it's likely the occurrences were not isolated.

A HAUNTING ON TYLER STREET

Submitted by an Anonymous Reader

There is a house on Tyler Street in Enid, Oklahoma, that is haunted. I do not want to reveal the address because it's a rental and I don't own the property, but what follows are some of the things that stand out in my memory.

There was one bedroom in the house that was always ten degrees lower than the rest of the house. We noticed this and thought it was odd so we kept a thermometer clock in there to be sure. We were right.

One night before he met me, my husband was living there alone. There were loud pounding footsteps a good portion of the night and it sounded like someone was banging their fists on the wall. A woman's voice came through the vents calling, "Help me!" Upon turning on the lights to investigate, my husband found an unexplained handprint on the wall.

Later, my husband was dating a woman with a two-year-old child. The little girl had the room that we later used as the weight room. After a while, she became very destructive, particularly at night. My husband started observing her play in her room from the living room. She appeared to be talking to someone invisible, only she would be looking high up, like she was conversing with a tall person. My husband sat her down for a talk.

He asked her who she was talking to. She said, "Mommy." He asked, "Who do you talk to when Mommy is not here?" She said, "I talk to you." He tried again, asking her, "Who do you talk to when Mommy and I are not in the room?" To his shock, she answered, "The dead people." He gamely went on and asked, "What do the dead people say?" She told him, "They don't like you and Mommy. They want to tie your hands up and do mean things to you."

I am not sure how he handled that one, but I know that he had the house blessed after that. That pretty much calmed that kind of "bad stuff" down to just annoying stuff.

When we married and I moved in, we used the room where the little girl used to talk to the dead people as a weight room. One night after exercising I turned off the radio and left the room. Later in the evening, my husband heard the radio stations changing and the music playing very softly. The radio had a knob tuner so you could see the needle move to different stations. He went in there and watched as the needle moved to an oldies station.

I also saw black "swirly" things when I turned out the lights. When I moved in, I had a really hard time adjusting, until my husband gave me a hint: if I turned on the TV, they would usually stay quiet. For some reason they did not like the TV.

My sister was staying with us one night and sleeping on the couch. We had brought home an antique clock that night. About 2:00 am, my sister awoke to see the clock being tossed in her direction. We found it laying face-down and it appeared to have turned a ninety-degree angle mid-air. We had left it sitting in a chair face-up when we went to bed.

Another night, my sister was sleeping on the couch again. She had not fallen asleep yet and she felt footsteps coming up from behind the couch. She looked and no one was there although she felt a strong presence in the room.

We experienced loud footsteps every night, like someone stomping through the kitchen right up to our bedroom door and we heard voices coming through the vents.

You could feel someone watching you when you were alone in the room. Sometimes the hair would stand up all over my body and sometimes I would get a cold chill. My husband would tell them to "back off" in a normal toned voice and after a while he could not feel them watching anymore.

After we moved out, I guess the landlord gave the new tenants gave our phone number because they called, asking questions. It turned out they had the same problems. They had a baby monitor hooked up and could also hear voices coming from that. I don't know who lives in the house now because it's been awhile since we moved out. I do suspect the landlord has a hard time renting the place.

MARY'S HOUSE
By Tammy Wilson

Weird things were happening at Mary's house. So weird, in fact, that she even called the police on one occasion.

Mary's daughter and her daughter's boyfriend had been living there with Mary. One night a man was seen so clearly they thought there was an intruder in the house and they immediately called the police. The police arrived and after they made sure no one was in the home and they checked to make sure all the doors and windows were secured, they basically told the occupants they must have been seeing things. It's not a big house and the likelihood of someone hiding and being undetected is pretty low.

Another time, Mary's daughter reported waking up and seeing a man standing over them while they slept. They were absolutely terrified. She and her boyfriend moved out of the house not too long after that.

Yet another night Mary heard the tapestry that hangs on the door to the guest room start swinging. Then she heard the door opening and slamming several times. She was completely alone in the house.

Mary did not know much about the house's history but she asked us to investigate it. We did a walkthrough and made notes and we took photographs and readings of all the rooms. We decided to leave the tape recorder and EMF detectors in the guest room where the man had been seen and the noises had been heard while we went into the other room to talk - pretending to just be visiting rather than "investigating." I have a theory that more things tend to happen when you are not expecting them to. So as we were chatting and laughing in the living room, we heard the EMF detector start squelching. It was odd to us to have an EMF meter randomly go off. We ran to the bedroom and of course, the video equipment was not filming for some reason. It never works right when you need it to! We were able to tape the EMF meter going off, but that wasn't enough to tell us what caused it to activate in the first place. There were no other noises on the tape to indicate what could have caused it.

Just for fun, we tried using dowsing rods. During our dowsing session in the bedroom with just three of us, Kathy, an Eerie Oklahoma team member, suggested asking if its name was Ben. We asked if his name was Ben and the rods indicated "no." I mentioned that I was getting an impression of "John" and Kathy said that was her initial impression as well, but that it seemed too common and so she went with Ben instead. We went ahead and asked if his name was John and the rods indicated "yes." Over the course of several dowsing sessions and a pendulum session, we discovered that Mary's visitor's name was John; that he passed away at an old age, and that he had lived in that house, but had not died there. We also discovered that he didn't like Mary. It was nothing personal; he didn't particularly want anyone living in his house.

Now, let me clarify - I thought this whole dowsing thing was going to be bunk and that we were just getting random indications. Dowsing rods have not been proven and are rarely used as an investigative tool by reputable teams and as I mentioned, we were just trying them out for a bit if fun. But they were consistent every time we asked the same questions throughout the evening. I truly thought that none of the answers would make sense in the grand scheme of things.

The following day, I researched the address using a search resource that licensed law enforcement agencies use to locate people. This source will list everyone who has lived at that address in the last several years and will list the months and years they lived there. It will also list their age and birth date. A big red "D" will appear next to their name if they are deceased.

When I ran Mary's address, there were twenty-eight results. There was one John. He had a big red "D" next to his name and he died when he was eighty-one. He was the ONLY one on the list with the red "D" and the only John. Coincidence? Maybe - but we don't think so.

DEAD WOMAN'S CROSSING
By Troy Taylor

One of the strangest tales of Oklahoma is the story of a place known as "Dead Woman's Crossing", an old river bridge that is located in a remote area near Weatherford. For years, stories circulated about a wooden bridge where the wheels of a wagon could still be heard turning if anyone was brave enough to go there late at night. People who lived in the area were familiar with the ghostly tale but always assumed that it was just a legend. Little did they know that this particular legend had a real-life murder tale behind it.

The story began on July 7, 1905 in Custer County, Oklahoma when Katy Dewitt James, a pleasant and well-liked young woman, left home and boarded a train to visit a cousin in Payne County. Although popular in the community, no one knew that Katy hid dark secrets from everyone. On the afternoon before she left Custer County, she had filed for divorce from her husband on the grounds of cruelty. This was a daring step for a woman of those times and Katy thought it best to put some distance between herself and her volatile husband. Her father, Henry, helped her to pack her things and he took her to the train himself. He watched from the platform as the train pulled out of the station. He had no idea that this was the last time that he would ever see his daughter alive.

Katy never arrived at her cousin's house and as far as anyone knew, disappeared from the face of the earth. After her father did not receive word from her for several weeks, he hired a detective named Sam Bartell to look for her. Bartell attempted to trace Katy's movements but found nothing until he reached Weatherford. Questioning some of the locals, he discovered that a woman matching Katy's description had stayed with a woman that she had met on the train. The woman was known to people in Weatherford as a "Mrs. Ham". She was a prostitute who owned a boarding house just off the main streets in the downtown area. Her real name was Fannie Norton.

According to what Bartell could find out, Katy and her child had stayed the night of July 7 in the home of William Moore, Fannie Norton's brother-in-law. On the morning of July 8, the two women and the baby had been seen leaving town in a buggy. Norton had mentioned to a worker at the livery stable that they would be back in about three hours. He overheard Norton telling Katy that they were going to Hydro, a nearby town, and would come back soon. The same stable hand reported that Norton had returned a little over two hours later -- and she had come back alone.

Bartell stayed on the trail and set off toward Hydro, questioning people along the way about any sightings of two women and a baby who had recently passed that way. Finally, he ran across a woman who had seen the buggy pass by. She added that she had seen them enter a field near Deer Creek and then pass back the same way about forty-five minutes later. When the buggy came back, only a women fitting Norton's description was in the buggy and she had the baby with her.

The detective continued to visit farms around the area and found more people who had encountered Fanny Norton on July 8. She had driven the buggy to a farm near Deer Creek and had left the baby with a small boy, telling him to give the baby to his mother to care for until she returned. Bartell was relieved to discover that the little girl was alive and well and still being cared for by the family. He immediately sent word to Henry Dewitt to let him know that he had found his granddaughter. Unfortunately, Bartell was given some startling information by the family. The woman who had been caring for the baby brought him the dress that the child had been wearing on the day that Norton had abandoned her. It was covered with blood. She also told him that her son had distinctly remembered seeing what also appeared to be blood splashed all over the side of the buggy when Norton had given him the baby.

Now worried, Bartell once again picked up Norton's trail and followed her across the state to Shawnee, where local police arrested her in a room that she had rented from the local butcher and his wife. When questioned as to the whereabouts of Katy James, she told a rambling, far-fetched tale about Katy meeting a man while out on the buggy ride and going away with him. Neither Bartell nor the police detectives were convinced by her story and did not believe that Katy would have abandoned her child with a woman that she hardly knew. Norton vehemently denied killing Katy, however, and she wept bitterly, allegedly because no one would believe her.

Later that evening, during a break in her interrogation, Bartell was out in the hallway talking to a reporter and Norton began to vomit. Heaving and gasping for air, she collapsed onto the floor and never recovered. It was determined that she had taken some sort of poison and the doctor said that he didn't think she had long to live. He was right -- Fannie Norton died early the next morning, never confessing about what had happened to Katy. Her death was ruled a suicide and since her body was unclaimed, she was buried in an unmarked grave in the Shawnee city cemetery.

The only person who knew where Katy might be was gone, but Sam Bartell refused to give up the search. Various rewards were posted by Henry Dewitt and even by the territorial governor. The search went on for more than a month before Katy was found. On August 31, a Weatherford man named G.W. Cornell came forward to collect the reward. He and his sons found her body while fishing along Deer Creek. The remains were badly decomposed, but the hair matched that of Katy's. Her clothing was recognizable and a gold ring was still on the corpse's finger. Her skull had been severed from the body and was lying a short distance away, close to where her hat was found under a pile of mud and debris.

Once the corpse was examined, a bullet hole was discovered behind the woman's right ear. It was believed to have come from the revolver that was found a short distance downstream -- a revolver that Fannie Norton's attorney positively identified as belonging to his late client. Investigators surmised that Norton had shot Katy while she was sitting in the buggy and then Katy had pitched forward, falling down into the creek bed below. The area was secluded and no one had seen anything and no one had heard the shot.

At the inquest, Katy's estranged husband, Martin Luther James, was called to testify. He was sarcastic on the stand and had never expressed any sorrow or concern about his wife and daughter's disappearance, or Katy's death. For this reason, many suspected him of having a hand in Katy's murder. However, there was no evidence of it and he had an alibi for his whereabouts at the time of her death. A grand jury later indicted Norton for murder, with robbery being the motive, although she had been dead for some weeks by the time the proceedings came to a conclusion.

Because a divorce decree had not been granted before her death, Martin James became the administrator of her rather substantial estate. Her father was very wealthy and had set up a trust for his daughter when she was a child. She had come of age not long before and had inherited a large sum of money, as well as land holdings and a working farm. James also petitioned for custody of his daughter and she was taken away from her grandfather and given back to him. Not long after, he sold the farm, liquidated Katy's accounts and vanished with his daughter. Whatever became of Martin James -- and Katy's little girl -- remains a complete mystery.

And this is not the only lingering mystery from this case. Who was Fannie Norton and why would she have murdered a woman that she barely knew? And if she did kill Katy because she wanted to rob her, then why leave the body with a gold ring still on her finger? Most of those who have looked into the case do not believe that Fannie acted alone in the murder of Katy Dewitt James. Most believe that she was hired to kill Katy by the estranged husband, Martin James, either to keep the divorce from becoming legal, to steal her estate, or most likely, for both reasons. If Fannie was a prostitute, as most in Weatherford believed, it is thought that perhaps James met her in her professional capacity and then made arrangements for Katy's murder. What really happened remains a mystery and the case remains unsolved.

One thing that was not a mystery to those who lived near Weatherford, however, was the fact that the bridge and riverbed where Katy had been killed was haunted. It was said that on moonlit nights, if one stood near the bridge, a visitor could hear the sound of a woman, believed to be Katy, calling out for her child. The story went on to say that anyone who stood beneath the wooden bridge could hear the sound of buggy wheels rolling across it, the impatient stamp of horse's hooves, a sudden cracking sound and then a splash as if something had been thrown from the bridge into the water below. It likely goes without saying that when examined, there was no sign of a buggy and nothing in the river beneath it. It came to be realized that this was a spectral re-playing of Katy's last moments on earth.

The old wooden bridge at what has become known as "Dead Woman's Crossing" has since been replaced by a large concrete structure but it remains an eerie place. In more recent years, the area below the bridge has become a popular gathering place for students and teenagers, who come to party and to soak up the ambience of a real-life haunting.

For years, most believed the story of the spectral buggy and the often reported cold spots beneath the bridge - where Katy's body allegedly decomposed - was nothing more than a spooky tale that had been cooked up by college students. It was a surprise for many of these people to discover that there was a true story at the heart of the legend. Given what really happened here in 1905, we have to perhaps think again before handily dismissing some of the legends that we hear because there just may be more to them than we think.

THE CARMEN HOME
By Tammy Wilson

"Cyclone Wrecked Business Portion of Carmen, Destroying Life and Property in its Course"

"Aline, O.T., May 23.-The town of Carmen, five miles north of here, was struck by a cyclone last evening about 7:30, and one-third of the buildings were destroyed, including the business portion. Two persons were killed and twenty more or less injured.

The storm came from the northwest and passed through the town mowing a swath about a block in width. The Methodist church was picked up bodily and set on the top of the parsonage, where it still remains. Entering the business streets the storm entirely demolished the Wismiller block, including the post office, Merrill's furniture store, Carmen drug store, Halstead meat market, Hendlight newspaper office and Wismiller's hardware store.

P.F. Brown, representing the Plano Machinery Company, of Wichita, was struck by flying timbers and killed instantly, his brains being found thirty feet from his body. Jacob Rader, who was walking with him at the time, jumped into a water tank and escaped injury.

Mrs. Wismiller, wife of the owner of the Wismiller block, was fatally injured, and died this evening.

The storm proceeded up Main Street, wrecking every building in its path. Every livery stable was destroyed, and lumber from the yards is scattered all over the town and vicinity. Three box cars of the Orient railroad, and the private car of the superintendent, were blown from the track, severely injuring a civil engineer.

Damage to property will reach $100,000 in the town, and reports indicate that this will be increased in the surrounding country.

Carmen is situated in the geographical center of Woods County, and is the present terminus of the Orient railway, about 30 miles south of the Kansas line. The population is reported to be 500 at present."

This story appeared May 24, 1903, in relation to the historic tornado that tore through Carmen, Oklahoma, ripping the small town apart. Oddly enough, Carmen is one of the few small railroad towns of Oklahoma that survived. Even though it has not grown a great deal in the last century, it has at least maintained its population in the range of five hundred, give or take a few people, whereas most of its contemporaries have long since vanished.

Years later another tornado swept through the town and destroyed the top floor and ornate roof of the Carmen Home. The Carmen Home (IOOF Home for Children) was opened in 1907 and was empty for ten or twelve years when it became the private residence of Jim and Naomi Davis in 1940. After that the Pentecostal Holiness Church purchased it around 1944 and made it into the Carmen Home for Elderly in 1954. The building was a nursing home for many years and it also served as a rehab-type facility for a short period of time before being left to sit empty on the barren plains. It is rumored to be haunted.

In November of 2004, we set out to investigate the old orphanage. We were met by several anxious locals, who told us no one went in there very often. Some of them even waited outside until we were done that evening. They all seemed to be more than a little spooked about the place but no one was too willing to say why. One woman, however, told us about her grandmother's days in the nursing home there.

This investigation was part of a cognitive research theory Eerie and GHOULI were working on. No one knew the building's history before we went. When we got there, we split up into teams, each team assigned to a separate zone in the building. The teams were sent through with notebooks and were asked to write down any impressions or feelings they had during the walkthrough. They were asked to not share their comments with other team members. After that, each team went through with their equipment and wrote down any unusual occurrences they experienced with the equipment. Both sets of numbers were given to one person to correlate to see if any of the impressions would match up with equipment occurrences and to see if different people were getting the same results.

At one point, the team had gathered in a common room where there were several chairs arranged in a circle. There weren't enough regular chairs, so Tonya sat in a wheelchair that was in the room. We were sitting in the circle talking and conducting an EVP session when Tonya's chair moved on its own! She said something to the effect of, "Oh my god this chair just moved!" and I snapped a picture of her startled reaction. Her feet were not touching the ground and her hands weren't near the wheels. Susie, a member of our team, saw it move completely on its own. It moved backward as if someone had pulled it.

Some time later, four of us decided to do a walkthrough in the basement. It was big, maze-like, and very dark. We spent some time in what was once the beauty shop. It was eerie because it looked as if everyone had just walked out one day and left everything; there were still hair clippings all over.

As we wandered down the dark hallways, we all got the feeling that we were being followed. Tonya began talking out loud to whoever was there and she got the impression that we should go find the piano. So we wandered some more and came to an old piano way back in a corner of a dead end. None of us knew it was there. While we were all standing there, there was a bright flash of light at the end of the hall. We all witnessed it then it was gone. We went upstairs to meet up with the others and I felt I

The Carmen Home (IOOF Home for Children), built in 1907

needed to tell Russell what I thought the person looked like who was following us. So I took him aside and gave him my description. Later he got a description from Tonya and they were almost exactly the same. We both felt it was an older woman who walked hunched over, wearing a housecoat-type garment, with short curly hair shuffling along behind us. Now, you may think that seems like a pretty generic description of someone in a nursing home, but the details down to the hair matched and it was a very strong impression. Normally I don't put a lot of stock into impressions, but this was a pretty interesting coincidence.

While on the main floor, Tonya at one time literally ran down the hall trying to get pictures of something she said she saw. She said she saw a bare leg from the knee down with a bit of a nightgown go around the corner, but it was gone when she got there.

During one point in the evening, several of the women who were mothers reported feeling a warm spot about waist level. We could feel it with our hands - and it was one of the coldest nights of the year. We wondered if perhaps the warm spot might have been the ghost of one of the orphan children. It was quite a bittersweet experience for us.

Considering the type of place the Carmen Home was, there were certainly deaths there, but nothing in its history tells of any mistreatment or unhappiness. There is a cemetery down the road that was made just for the orphanage and there are about twelve children buried there.

As far as we know, the home has since been purchased and people are living there. The current owners no longer allow investigations in the building.

GHOSTLAHOMA
Over 100 Years of Oklahoma's Haunted History

Ghostlahoma is a collection of "true" ghost stories throughout Oklahoma. They have been collected over the years by paranormal investigators and para-historians, Tonya Hacker and Tammy Wilson. Some of the stories have been submitted by the people who experienced them and some happened to the authors themselves. This book is just the tip of the iceberg when it comes to covering the haunted history of the Sooner State and we hope to continue bringing you chilling accounts of times gone by, bumps in the night, local legends, and haunted houses in Oklahoma.

Everyone has a story and we would like to hear yours. If you have a true Oklahoma ghost story to share, please send it to either one of us to be included in the next volume of Ghostlahoma stories.

tonya.hacker@gmail.com or **tammylynwilson@gmail.com**

Thank you for reading.
Happy haunting!
Tammy & Tonya

ABOUT THE AUTHORS

Tammy Wilson

Married mother of 4, Tammy Wilson lives in Enid, Oklahoma. She loves reading and watching movies cuddled up with her husband, Marty, on the loveseat. She's especially a sucker for scary movies!

Wilson is the founder of Eerie Oklahoma, a paranormal investigation team that researches and investigates haunted places all over Oklahoma. Along with her co-author, Tonya Hacker, she hosts the internet radio show "Ghost Divas Live!" and is an avid blogger in the paranormal community.

Wilson continually looks for ways to make what they do interesting, entertaining, and accessible to the public. She conducts a ghost town tour of four northern Oklahoma counties and is working on tours for other counties as well. She is very involved with her children and her community and is the organizer and co-conspirator of Enid's down town Halloween festival, Scare on the Square.

Wilson loves learning about new things and is likely working on a different project every time you talk to her, although her main passion lies in keeping Oklahoma history alive through the stories and legends of the great state and its wonderfully colorful people.

Tonya' Hacker

Tonya Hacker is a single mother of two residing in Moore, Oklahoma, a suburb of Oklahoma City. She has been interested in the unexplained her entire life. Years after outgrowing her favorite pesky ghost chasing cartoons she ended up living in a real haunted house. The experiences Hacker had while living in the home encouraged her to not only start researching ghosts but it also made her realize her passion for the paranormal was much deeper than helping others make sense of their unearthly guests. They encouraged her to start writing about the stories behind the haunts. Hacker is an avid blogger in the paranormal field and a host of a very well known internet radio show, "Ghost Divas Live!"

Her knowledge of "things that go bump in the night" has set her on a new path which is history and travel. After staying in a haunted Bed & Breakfast and dining in rumored haunted places, she realized that she enjoyed the adventures of travel even more than researching. She enjoys entering locations as a guest and thrives on learning the stories, the history, and the haunting tales that are attached to them. Hacker enjoys relaxing and experiencing the haunting as a regular person, not a paranormal investigator.

Some of her favorite haunts in the Sooner state include such places as the Skirvin Hotel and the Bricktown area. Hacker is excited about writing more Ghostlahoma series and has already been contacted to write about more places that accessible to the public. Travel, tourism and history are the main focus of her writing and she is excited about being able to explore Oklahoma's other side. Her children, Tegan and Airis, have been surrounded by history and tales of the past since the day they were born. She hopes they will keep the legends alive with the spooky tales from the great state of Ghostlahoma!

ABOUT WHITECHAPEL PRESS

Whitechapel Productions Press is a division of Dark Haven Entertainment and a small press publisher, specializing in books about ghosts and hauntings. Since 1993, the company has been one of America's leading publishers of supernatural books and has produced such best-selling titles as **"The Ghost Hunter's Guidebook", Sex & the Supernatural, Dead Men Do Tell Tales, Spirits of the Civil War** and many others. With nearly a dozen different authors producing high quality books on all aspects of ghosts, hauntings and the paranormal, Whitechapel Press has made its mark with America's ghost enthusiasts.

You can visit Whitechapel Productions Press online and browse through our selection of ghostly titles, plus get information on ghosts and hauntings, haunted history, spirit photographs, information on ghost hunting and much more, by visiting the internet website at:
WWW. DARK HAVEN ENTERTAINMENT.COM

Ghosts of Route 66: History & Hauntings of America's Mother Road
by Troy Taylor & Kathy Weiser

www.ingramcontent.com/pod-product-compliance
Lightning Source LLC
LaVergne TN
LVHW022111080426
835511LV00007B/757